Future of Business and Finance

The Future of Business and Finance book series features professional works aimed at defining, describing and charting the future trends in these fields. The focus is mainly on strategic directions, technological advances, challenges and solutions which may affect the way we do business tomorrow, including the future of sustainability and governance practices. Mainly written by practitioners, consultants and academic thinkers, the books are intended to spark and inform further discussions and developments.

More information about this series at http://www.springer.com/series/16360

Tankiso Moloi • Tshilidzi Marwala

Artificial Intelligence and the Changing Nature of Corporations

How Technologies Shape Strategy and Operations

Springer

Tankiso Moloi
School of Accounting
University of Johannesburg
Johannesburg, South Africa

Tshilidzi Marwala
University of Johannesburg
Johannesburg, South Africa

ISSN 2662-2467 ISSN 2662-2475 (electronic)
Future of Business and Finance
ISBN 978-3-030-76312-1 ISBN 978-3-030-76313-8 (eBook)
https://doi.org/10.1007/978-3-030-76313-8

This Springer imprint is published by the registered company Springer Nature Switzerland AG.
The registered company address is: Gewerbestrasse 11, 6330 Cham, Switzerland

Preface

This book examines how various forms of artificial intelligence (AI) could shape a firms' strategy. To assess how AI is likely going to shape firm strategy, the book confines itself to AI forms such as machine learning (ML), natural language processing (NLP), and robotic process automation (RPA).

After the introductory chapter, the book discusses a high-level overview of artificial intelligence in Chap. 2. It discusses strategy conceptualisation and formulation in Chap. 3. Chapter 4 discusses strategy implementation.

Chapter 5 discusses machine learning as a form of artificial intelligence. It provides an understanding of machine learning as a starting point. It further considers how machine learning (ML) could be used to shape strategy and strategy implementation.

Chapter 6 discusses natural language processing as a form of artificial intelligence. It provides an understanding of natural language processing (NLP). The chapter further postulates how the NLP could be used to shape strategy and strategy implementation.

Chapter 7 discusses robotics and robotics process automation as a form of artificial intelligence. Its aim is to determine how robotic process automation (RPA) could be used to shape strategy and strategy implementation. Chapter 8 provides a synopsis of the book.

This book is an interesting resource for graduate students, researchers, business executives, and artificial intelligence practitioners interested in strategy theories and artificial intelligence.

Johannesburg, South Africa
March 2021

Tankiso Moloi
Tshilidzi Marwala

Acknowledgments

We would like to thank Dr. Denhere and Dr. Mhlanga for their assistance with gathering write-ups on some of the literature considered. They are post-doctoral research fellows in the School of Accounting.

March 2021.

School of Accounting, University of Johannesburg
Johannesburg, South Africa
Tankiso Moloi

University of Johannesburg
Johannesburg, South Africa
Tshilidzi Marwala

Contents

1 Introduction to Artificial Intelligence and the Nature of a Firm: Implications to Strategy and Strategy Implementation

1.1 Introduction

Early economics literature had a profound belief that one of the core resources, if not the most principal resource, was the human resource. We have repeatedly seen the argument that the most critical resource for any form of organisation, be it in the country or the firm, is 'its people'. Therefore, it was not a surprise that before the 1930s, the classical economic view was that businesses should hire employees. This could be done when and if businesses required them for specific tasks (Moloi, 2018).

It is equally not a surprise that in 1937, Ronald Coase put forward a compelling argument in *The Nature of the Firm*, observing that firms in the Detroit region grew only so long as it was cheaper for them to complete additional parts of the production process in-house rather than resort to the open market. With labour as an example, Ronald Coase argued that transaction costs and search-related complications associated with the procurement of resources at short notice could be problematic for firms. As such, his view was that it would make sense to keep employees on the company's books.

It would seem Ronald Coase feared that negotiations in an open market would likely increase the unit costs of labour, causing the production of an item to be expensive. Coase may also have feared that if the demand for a firm's product was to increase, at the same time that the firm did not have sufficient labour to meet production requirements, the firm would either lose business to its competitors or may be forced to bid for these employees in the open market, and they would join that particular firm at a high cost.

Perhaps Coase had in mind what in today's terms we refer to as competitive pricing. In order for the firm to price its product competitively, it has to manage its costs. According to Chappelow (2019), competitive pricing refers to the process of selecting strategic price points. This allows the firm to best take advantage of a product- or service-based market relative to the competition.

T. Moloi, T. Marwala, *Artificial Intelligence and the Changing Nature of Corporations*, Future of Business and Finance,
https://doi.org/10.1007/978-3-030-76313-8_1

Furthermore, this pricing method is often used by firms that are selling similar products. The distinguishing factor is then the pricing aspect since services can vary from one firm to the next whereas the attributes of a product remain similar. Accordingly, a competitive pricing strategy would ordinarily be used once a price for a product or service has reached a level of equilibrium. Equilibrium in this regard occurs when a product has been on the market for a long time and when there are many substitutes for the product.

We note that the rise of institutional shareholders in the 1990s began to undermine the Coasean doctrine, as these shareholders encouraged businesses to outsource certain non-core functions. An example here would be of what these institutional shareholders would demand in a mining company, in which the core functionaries would be geological surveyors, miners, engineers and similar functionaries. Due to the nature of mining, operations would typically be based in remote areas where housing is required.

Since builders were not necessarily seen as the core of the mining business, conventional wisdom, according to institutional shareholders in the 1990s, would be that employees had to be outsourced for a project surrounding the development of houses for a mining company. The critical point, though, is that the work would be outsourced to another company that would have the workforce to undertake such a project.

Clearly, for a long time, firms have operated within certain boundaries. These boundaries include the 'in-house production as envisaged by Coase', having operations in a specific region or country, compliance with certain legislation applicable to regions of application, facing uncertainties relating to regions where they operate and raising capital in traditional capital markets among other boundaries. The most essential resource was the human capital. As new technologies took hold, it affected the human resources.

To demonstrate this, Aubert et al. (2006) investigated the relationships between new technologies, innovative workplace practices and the age structure of the workforce in a sample of French firms. Their findings are important in demonstrating the impact of technologies on human capital. Their results demonstrated that the wage-bill share of older workers was lower in innovative firms and that the opposite held for younger workers.

According to Aubert et al. (2006), the age bias affected both men and women in a sense that new technologies essentially affected older workers through reduced hiring opportunities. Their study further found that firms' innovations mainly increased older employees' probability of exiting the company, which decreased much less for younger workers following readjustment.

Both the Ronald Coase fear that negotiations in an open market would likely increase the unit costs of labour, causing the production of an item to be expensive, and the rise of institutional shareholders in the 1990s, which encouraged businesses to outsource certain non-core functions, hinged on the idea that labour was an important aspect of the production process. Aubert, Caroli and Roger's (Aubert et al., 2006) investigation and the subsequent findings in French companies undermine the concept of labour as an important aspect in a firm.

The 2019 debate between Elon Musk and Jack Ma, who are deemed the titans of technology, emphasises the changed role of a human being, given the advances in artificial intelligence (Sarmah, 2019). As AI advances, what becomes clear in this debate is that technology 'will inevitably change the way we live and work'.

We know that before the COVID-19 pandemic, the world was already changing rapidly. According to Birkinshaw (2018), artificial intelligence was already playing a major role by assisting many firms to exploit their existing sources of advantage. The existing sources of advantage were exploited through process automation, improved problem-solving or quality assurance. In addition, AI was also beginning to be useful in exploring new sources of advantage.

Moloi and Marwala (2020) concur with the above but bring in a broader perspective. They argue that not only has technology had a huge impact on firms; it has also had impact on almost all aspects of life, such as economies, or even politics, among other aspects. Human life, economies and politics have all been affected by the rapid changes brought by developments in information technology (Harari, 2018). In their treatise, Moloi and Marwala (2020) posit that technological advances allowed humanity to discover powerful energy sources. It allowed humans to discover faster modes of transportation, goods and services, improved the speed at which we communicate and landed human beings on the moon. There is now even an attempt to send a mission to Mars. In the same vein, advances in technology have allowed other businesses to continue to operate, even amid the lockdowns implemented in response to the COVID-19 pandemic.

1.2 The Pandemic and the Great Acceleration of Technology Utilisation

As the world changed, it would seem that firms and individuals within firms were caught between leveraging the advances brought about by technology and keeping certain aspects of the firm in a traditional form. For instance, in most companies, meetings had to be attended physically in the boardrooms, even though virtual meeting platforms had been available for some time.

Then the great COVID-19 pandemic descended on humanity towards the end of 2019. This led to the majority of governments confining their citizens due to the fear that the virus would spread and the anticipation that the hospitals would not cope. In most parts of the world, businesses such as gymnasiums, restaurants, nightclubs, bars and casinos all had to shut down or work with minimal staff members.

However, businesses that do not necessarily require physical presence continued to operate under these circumstances. Meetings, workshops or labs were swiftly moved to the virtual space. There has been an intense utilisation of technologies such as Google Meet, CISCO WEBEX, Zoom, Microsoft Teams and Skype among other technologies.

In the same period, we also witnessed the property market business moving towards advanced technology such as 3D. The Financial Times (2020) reports of a house in central London that was sold to an overseas buyer for six million pounds.

The buyer of the property had never set foot in the house to examine it. They relied on technology and had confidence that it would deliver on their needs. The decision was made based on virtual walkthroughs made possible by 3D cameras.

As fear gripped human beings to the degree that even shopping for groceries posed the risk of contracting the deadly coronavirus, there has been a shift towards e-commerce; consumers purchase their grocery items online and have them delivered directly to their doors. We witnessed television anchors anchoring their shows via these technological tools. Interviews were conducted through these connected technologies, and the viewer at home has not had to suffer disruptions in programming.

Based on our examples above, it is apparent that the rock on which the firm was initially thought, and had built its foundation, has shifted, and advances in technology are at the forefront of this shift. The question then is: How will this shift shape firm strategy and strategy implementation in the future? We believe that a firm's nature as previously understood and articulated needs to be revisited, particularly the aspect of strategy and strategy implementation. As Birkinshaw (2018) has argued, this is because firms do not only manage the day to day trade-offs between exploitation and exploration but also need to manage the trade-offs over time.

During the process of managing the trade-offs between the short term and the long term, which is vital for the sustainability of a firm, many decisions have to be made. Birkinshaw's (2018) view is that technology such as AI is not equipped to make such a judgement. Our position is that judgement requires information. The ability of AI to harness massive amounts of data is an important aspect of the management of trade-offs, particularly in the long term where certain scenarios may be uncertain.

Instead of relying on human resources as an important aspect of the firm's processes, to be successful firms will need to incorporate advanced data analytics in the strategic planning and incorporate advanced data analytics and some aspect of automating the strategy execution (business processes/operations). There have been breakthroughs in deep learning recently. These breakthroughs have made the interaction between AI, strategy and operations a vital topic for firms (LeCun et al., 2015; Silver et al., 2016).

1.3 Artificial Intelligence

Moloi and Marwala (2020) point out that literature has not attempted to utilise the current technological advances to modernise economics and finance theories that are fundamental in the decision-making process for allocating scarce resources, among other things. They argue that simulated intelligence allows machines to act like humans. Therefore, it can further anticipate events better than human beings can.

In essence, Moloi and Marwala (2020) argue that artificial intelligence revolutionised specific economics and finance theories, owing to its ability to handle massive datasets. Similarly, literature is very thin on how emerging technologies such as AI could shape the firm's strategy and subsequent strategy implementation.

What is this AI that allows machines to act like humans and even anticipate events better than humans, thanks to its ability to handle massive datasets? What is this AI that allows machines to act like humans and is expected to have a crucial role in shaping successful or unsuccessful firms in the future? How can it reshape the firm strategy and operations, providing a competitive advantage to deploying it?

Various definitions of AI exist. Monett and Lewis (2018) argue that the reason for the existence of various definitions of AI is that 'theories in and around AI and the goal of AI have been the source of much confusion. The confusion is within the field of AI and the general public'.

According to Marr (2018), AI refers to the theory and development of computer systems that can perform tasks that typically require human intelligence. Examples of the tasks include visual perception, speech recognition, decision-making and translation between languages (Marr, 2018).

For Copeland (2020), AI is a digital computer or computer-controlled robot that performs tasks that would commonly be associated with intelligent human beings. This could involve developing systems equipped with intellectual processes that characterise humans, such as the ability to reason, discover meaning, learn from experience or generalise.

An example of similar definitions of AI is that of Merriam-Webster (2018), where AI is seen as the field of computer science committed to solving intellectual problems that are analogous to human intelligence, such as learning, problem-solving and pattern recognition. This field of science deals with the simulation of cognitive behaviour in computers. In simple terms, AI can be described as a technique that is used to make computers intelligent (Marwala, 2007, 2009).

There exist various forms of artificial intelligence. This book examines how various forms of AI could shape a firm's strategy. To assess how AI is likely going to shape the firm strategy, the book confines itself to AI forms such as machine learning (ML), natural language processing (NLP) and robotic process automation (RPA).

1.3.1 A Brief Introduction to Machine Learning

Marwala (2018) explains machine learning as a statistical approach to making intelligent machines. An example of ML is a neural network. Therefore, a neural network is based on the human brain's functioning through neurons and how these fire electrical signals to transmit information.

According to Edwards (2018), ML is one of the most influential and powerful technologies in today's world. ML is a tool for turning information into knowledge (Edwards, 2018). ML is different from the traditional software engineering that combined human created rules with data to create answers to a problem.

The difference is that ML uses data and answers to discover the rules behind a problem (Chollet, 2017). In essence, ML techniques are used to automatically find the valuable underlying patterns within complex data that human beings could otherwise struggle to discover. Furthermore, the hidden patterns and knowledge about a specific problem within data can be used to predict future events. Using data, ML can also perform all kinds of complex decision-making (Alpaydin, 2020).

Earlier, we argued that the ability of AI to harness massive amounts of data is an important aspect of managing trade-offs that most firms often face, particularly in the long term where certain scenarios may be uncertain. As Alpaydin (2020) posits, ML techniques are an automatic way used to find the valuable underlying patterns within complex data that human beings could otherwise struggle to discover. Furthermore, the hidden patterns and knowledge about a specific problem within data can be used to predict future events. In strategic decisions, firms can derive the ML advantage to understand patterns within complex data. Firms could also benefit from the prediction power of complex ML techniques.

Advances in technology mean that for firms to be successful, there will be a need to incorporate advanced data analytics in the strategic planning and to incorporate advanced data analytics and some aspect of automating in the strategy execution (business processes/operations). In this regard, this book explores the concept of ML in the context of the firm's strategy and strategy implementation. In this context, we explore the following questions:

- How can ML shape the firm strategy?
- How can ML be used to provide a competitive advantage to the firms deploying it?

1.3.2 A Brief Introduction to Natural Language Processing

According to Reshamwala et al. (2013), natural language processing (NLP) is 'a branch of computer science, AI and linguistics that focuses on the interactions between computers and human (natural) language'. Garbade (2018) provides a similar definition in which the NLP is viewed as 'a technology used to assist computers to understand humans' natural language'.

At its core, the NLP is used to express human knowledge and emotions and to transmit responses to other people in different forms of communication. According to Garbade (2018), the utmost objective of NLP is to read, decode, comprehend and make sense of the human languages. This sense may contain valuable information for decision-making. Heller (2019) posits that the NLP is currently one of the significant successful application areas of deep learning.

It was earlier indicated that advances in technology mean that for firms to be successful, there will be a need to incorporate advanced data analytics in the strategic planning and incorporate advanced data analytics and some aspect of automating the strategy execution (business processes/operations). As the strategy is implemented by various operations within the firm, it is important to evaluate its successes and challenges on an ongoing basis to ensure timely intervention. Since the NLP is used to express human knowledge and emotions and to transmit responses to other people in different forms of communication, this book explores the concept of NLP in the context of the firm's strategy and strategy implementation. In this context, we explore the following questions:

- How can NLP shape firm's strategy?
- How can the NLP be used to provide a competitive advantage associated with agility of timely intervention to those firms deploying it?

1.3.3 A Brief Introduction to Robotic Process Automation

According to GRANTA (2017), the main difference between robotics and automation is that robots are a piece of equipment that can perform a variety of tasks with programming, while automation is a term used for special purpose machines or systems that are designed to perform a specific task.

Brooks (1991) posits that robotics is the intersection of science, engineering and technology. This intersection produces machines called robots. Robots substitute for or replicate human actions. Accordingly, robots can consist of all sort of mechanical construction. As such, the mechanical aspect of a robot allows it to complete tasks in the environment for which it is designed. For example, the Mars 2020 Rover's wheels are individually motorised and made of titanium tubing that help it firmly grip the harsh terrain of the red planet (Wiens et al., 2017; Williford et al., 2018).

The robotic process automation (RPA) refers to the use of smart software. These smart software are used to carry out manual, repeatable and time-consuming tasks efficiently. Ordinarily, these tasks are performed by people (PWC South Africa, 2020). Boulton (2018) views the RPA as an application of technology, governed by business logic and structured inputs since it can be seen as a process that ensures efficient unison and design of business models, strategy, process, data, humans and robots. In this context, we explore the following questions:

- How can the RPA shape the firm's strategy?
- How can the RPA be used to provide a competitive advantage to those firms deploying it?

1.4 Themes of the Book

This book is entitled *Artificial Intelligence and the Changing Nature of the Firm: Implications to Strategy and Strategy Implementation*. It explores the central question under investigation: How does AI change the firm, especially the strategy and strategy implementation? For the firm to be sustainable over the long term, it has to have the edge or competitive advantage; otherwise, its competitors will squeeze it. Can firms use AI to derive this advantage? How can they do this? As indicated, the emphasis of the book is on ML, NLP and RPA.

To address the central question, we explore the concept of AI by providing a detailed background of what AI is. This is followed by the exploration of the firm's strategy, its implementation and the challenges often faced. Each form of AI, namely, ML, NLP and RPA, is then addressed separately, emphasising competitive advantage to those firms deploying it. The chapters of this book are organised as follows:

Chapter 1 provided a high-level introduction to AI and the nature of the firm, with specific emphasis on strategy and strategy implementation. We indicated in this chapter that our focus in the book is on three forms of AI, which are ML, NLP and the RPA.

Chapter 2 introduces AI. A high-level overview of AI is provided. It discusses the early days of AI, and this is followed by a discussion of significant developments in AI that followed the early slow start. Chapter 2 further provides some definitions of AI. What is evident in the discussion of definitions is that there is no standard definition of AI. The chapter then discusses the difference between weak and strong AI. Finally, it outlines the current developments and discusses some of the key modern-day AI technologies.

In Chap. 3, a point is made that strategy has long existed within living organisms. The strategy as a concept emanated from the need of the people to defeat their adversaries. This chapter provides a high-level overview of strategy. It discusses the historical account of strategy, followed by a discussion aimed at understanding the concept of strategy. The chapter further outlines and discusses processes that firms ought to engage in as they formulate strategy.

Chapter 4 discusses strategy implementation. It highlights some key definitions of strategy implementation. Following the definitions, a brief distinction between strategy implementation and strategy execution is considered. Some activities in strategy implementation are also outlined, and some factors that firms need to consider as they implement strategies are discussed. The last part of the chapter outlines the typical pitfalls and mitigations for successful strategy implementation.

Chapter 5 provides an overview of the concept of ML. This is followed by a discussion of the growing influence of ML. The forms of ML are also outlined, and a brief overview of deep learning is presented. The final part of the chapter explores ML in strategy and strategy implementation.

Chapter 6 discusses NLP as a form of AI. The chapter provides a high-level understanding of the NLP. It further hypothesises how the NLP could be used to shape strategy and strategy implementation within the firm.

Chapter 7 discusses the RPA as a form of AI. It provides considerations as to how the RPA could be used to shape strategy and strategy implementation within the firm.

Chapter 8 provides a synopsis of the book.

1.5 Key Points

- Firms have operated within certain boundaries.
- Firms, and individuals within those firms, are caught between leveraging the advances brought about by technology and keeping certain aspects of the firm in a traditional form.
- As the great pandemic (COVID-19) descended on humanity towards the end of 2019, most governments responded by confining their citizens due to the fear that the virus was to spread and that hospitals would not cope.
- Firms that had begun to explore the use of technology switched to remote working, and those that were not ready were suddenly facing an existential threat.
- The changes driven by technological advances indicate that the nature of the firm needs to be revisited.
- Literature is very thin on how emerging technologies such as the various forms of AI could shape firm strategy.
- Firms can derive advantage from understanding patterns within complex data. Firms could benefit from the prediction power of complex ML techniques.
- The advances in technology mean that for firms to be successful, there will be need to incorporate advanced data analytics in the strategic planning and to incorporate advanced data analytics and some aspects of automating strategy implementation.
- NLP is used to express human knowledge and emotions and to transmit responses to other people in different forms of communication. The NLP could be an important technology in monitoring and evaluating the strategy execution. It can do this by extracting human knowledge and emotions, across the firm as part of evaluating successes and challenges, so that there can be timely intervention.
- RPA can be seen as a process that ensures efficient unison and design of business models, strategy, process, data, humans and robots.
- These AI technologies could be an important aspect of competitive advantage to those firms deploying them.

References

Alpaydin, E. (2020). *Introduction to machine learning* (4th ed.). Cambridge, MA: The MIT Press.

Aubert, P., Caroli, E., & Roger, M. (2006). New technologies, firm and age: Firm-level evidence. *The Economic Journal, 116*(509), 73–93.

Birkinshaw, J. (2018). What's the purpose of companies in the age of AI? *Harvard Business Review*. Available from https://hbr.org/2018/08/whats-the-purpose-of-companies-in-the-age-of-ai

Boulton, C. (2018). *What is RPA? A revolution in business process automation*. Available from https://www.cio.com/article/3236451/what-is-rpa-robotic-process-automation-explained.html

Brooks, R. A. (1991). New approaches to robotics. *Science, 253*(5025), 1227–1232.

Chappelow, J. (2019). *Competitive pricing*. Available from https://www.investopedia.com/terms/c/competitive-pricing.asp

Chollet, F. (2017). *Deep learning with Python. Shelter Island Manning*. New York: Manning Publications Company.

Copeland, B. J. (2020). *What is artificial intelligence?* Available at http://www.alanturing.net/turing_archive/pages/Reference%20Articles/What%20is%20AI.html

Edwards, G. (2018). *Machine learning: An introduction*. Available from https://www.towardsdatascience.com/machine-learning-an-introduction-23b84d51e6d0

Garbade, M. J. (2018). *A simple introduction to natural language processing*. Available from https://wwwbecominghuman.ai/a-simple-introduction-to-natural-language-processing-ea66a1747b32

GRANTA. (2017). *What is the difference between automation and robotics?* Available from https://www.granta-automation.co.uk/news/what-is-the-difference-between-automation-and-robotics/

Harari, Y. N. (2018). *21 Lessons for the 21st century* (1st ed.). Vintage Publishers.

Heller, M. (2019). *What is natural language processing? AI for speech and text*. Available from https://www.infoworld.com/article/3398696/what-si-natural-language-processing-ai-for-speech-and-text.html

LeCun, Y., Bengio, Y., & Hinton, G. (2015). Deep learning. *Nature, 521*, 436–444.

Marr, B. (2018). *The key definitions of artificial intelligence (AI) that explain its importance*. Available from https://www.forbes.com/sites/bernardmarr/2018/02/14/the-key-definitions-of-artificial-intelligence-ai-that-explain-its-importance/?sh=7c079d514f5d

Marwala, T. (2007). *Computational intelligence for modelling complex systems*. Delhi: Research India Publications.

Marwala, T. (2009). *Computational intelligence for missing data imputation, estimation, and management: Knowledge optimization techniques*. Pennsylvania: IGI Global.

Marwala, T. (2018). *Handbook of machine learning: Foundation of artificial intelligence*. World Scientific Publication.

Merriam-Webster. (2018). *Artificial intelligence*. Available at https://www.merriamwebster.com/dictionary/artificial%20intelligence#:~:text=1%20%3A%20a%20branch%20of%20computer,to%20imitate%20intelligent%20human%20behavior

Moloi, T. (2018). *Get ready for the Fourth Industrial Revolution*. Available from https://www.iol.co.za/sundayindependent/analysis/get-ready-for-the-fourth-industrial-revolution-16209139

Moloi, T., & Marwala, T. (2020). *Artificial intelligence in economics and finance theories*. Publisher: Springer. isbn:978-3-030-42961-4.

Monett, D., & Lewis, C. W. P. (2018). Getting clarity by defining artificial intelligence - A survey. In V. C. Muller (Ed.), *Philosophy and theory of artificial intelligence 2017* (pp. 212–214). Berlin: Springer.

PWC South Africa. (2020). *Robotic process automation*. Available from https://www.pwc.co.za/en/services/advisor/robotic-process-automation.html

Reshamwala, A., Pawar, P., & Mishra, D. (2013). Review on natural language processing. *Engineering Science and Technology: An International Journal, 3*(1), 113–116.

Sarmah, H. (2019). Elon Musk vs Jack Ma: *When two tech titans clashed over AI at China summit*. Accessed from https://analyticsindiamag.com/elon-musk-vs-jack-ma-when-two-tech-titans-clashed-over-ai-at-china-summit/

Silver, D., Huang, A., Maddison, C. J., Guez, A., Sifre, L., van den Driessche, G., Schrittwieser, J., Antonoglou, I., Panneershelvam, V., Lanctot, M., Dieleman, S., Grewe, D., Nham, J., Kalchbrenner, N., Sutskever, I., Lillicrap, T., Leach, M., Kavukcuoglu, K., Graepel, T., & Hassabis, D. (2016). Mastering the game of Go with deep neural networks and tree search. *Nature, 529*, 484–489.

Wiens, R. C., Maurice, S., & Perez, F. (2017). *The SuperCam remote sensing instrument suite for the Mars 2020 rover mission: A preview*. Spectroscopy, 32(LA-UR-17-26876).

Williford, K. H., Farley, K. A., Stack, K. M., Allwood, A. C., Beaty, D., Beegle, L. W., & Hecht, M. H. (2018). *The NASA Mars 2020 rover mission and the search for extraterrestrial life*. In From Habitability to Life on Mars (pp. 275–308). Elsevier.

A High-Level Overview of Artificial Intelligence: Historical Overview and Emerging Developments

2

2.1 Introduction

Chapter 1 provided a high-level introduction to artificial intelligence and the nature of the firm, with specific emphasis on strategy and strategy execution. We indicated that our focus is on three forms of AI, namely, ML, NLP and RPA. This chapter provides a high-level overview on AI.

Historically, AI came into the spotlight through the work done by the United Kingdom and the United States. In the United Kingdom, Alan Turing worked towards, and was successful in, developing a machine, which was called the *Bombe*. The *Bombe* was an essential tool during World War II as it allowed Great Britain (GB) to decipher the codes sent between the command centres of the German army.

In order to provide a high-level overview, this chapter discusses the early days of AI in Sect. 2.2. This is followed in Sect. 2.3 by a discussion of major developments in AI following the early slow start. Section 2.4 provides some definitions of AI. Section 2.5 discusses the differences between weak and strong AI. Finally, Sect. 2.7 outlines current developments and discusses some of the key modern-day AI technologies.

2.2 The Early Days of AI

In 1950, Turing put together and published *Computing Machinery and Intelligence*, and it became a seminal work. At this point, it is important pause and note that the term AI had not been coined. In *Computing Machinery and Intelligence*, Turing (1950) proposed a way to create intelligent machines. He further proposed how machines can be tested for their intelligence. This was to be later known as the Turing test. Essentially, the Turing test can be explained as follows: if a human is interacting with a machine, but he/she is unable to determine whether he/she is

T. Moloi, T. Marwala, *Artificial Intelligence and the Changing Nature of Corporations*, Future of Business and Finance,
https://doi.org/10.1007/978-3-030-76313-8_2

interacting with a machine or a human being, then that machine is viewed as intelligent.

On the other side of the Atlantic Ocean, in the United States, the concept of AI was inspired by science fiction. Haenlein and Kaplan (2019) suggest that the science fiction known as *Runaround* created by Isaac Asimov was an inspiration for AI. *Runaround* tells a story of a robot that two engineers created. Three laws govern this robot, and these are as follows:

- A robot may not injure a human being or, through inaction, allow a human being to come to harm.
- A robot must obey the orders given to it by human beings except where such orders would conflict with the first law.
- A robot must protect its existence as long as such protection does not conflict with the first or second law (Smarzo, 2017).

Smarzo (2017) has since added the fourth law of robotics. In it, Smarzo (2017) points to the fact that when the robots first emerged, the relationship was one sided, and it was favouring human beings. Human beings told robots what to do, and robots just complied. Advances in AI are redefining this relationship. These advances have led to machines closing the gap and almost becoming equals in a certain number of tasks that human beings perform.

Essentially, the fourth law of robotics is that machines can make decisions and change 'their minds'. As Smarzo (2017) posits, in future, say the self-driving cars are now widely available, there will be situations where these cars 'will have to make life-and-death decisions regarding which humans to save, and which humans to kill'. Reflecting on this, it is clear that the first law (a robot may not injure a human being or, through inaction, allow a human being to come to harm) as envisaged in *Runaround* will no longer hold.

According to Haenlein and Kaplan (2019), *Runaround* inspired generations of scientists in robotics, AI and computer science. AI came to the mainstream academic discipline in the 1950s. Haenlein and Kaplan (2019) indicate that even though AI is one of the oldest academic disciplines, 'it had remained an area of relative scientific obscurity and limited practical interest for over half a century'. The reasons AI remained an area of academic obscurity are not clear; however, based on the definition that Haenlein and Kaplan (2019) advanced, which describes AI as a data-based system, the reasons could be computing power and lack of access to data.

In addition to this, early computers could not store commands. They only executed them. In essence, as Anyoha (2017) indicates, computers could be told what to do. The problem was that these early computers could not remember what they did. The ability of computers to store commands is a prerequisite for intelligence. Another early challenge in the computing world was that computers were unaffordable. To lease a computer, Anyoha (2017) estimates that the lessee had to pay approximately US$200K on monthly basis. Given this, there were very few institutions that could afford computer equipment.

As indicated earlier, the term AI was not coined until the late 1950s. This happened at a conference with a theme *Dartmouth Summer Research Project on Artificial Intelligence* (*DSRPAI*). The conference took place in one of US prestigious schools, the Dartmouth College based in New Hampshire. It was attended by luminaries such as John McCarthy, Marvin Minsky and Claude Shannon. Accordingly, this conference was funded by one of America's richest families, namely, the Rockefeller family through the Rockefeller Foundation.

2.3 Major Developments in AI

The major challenge experienced earlier that computers could not store commands, only executed them but could not remember what they did, was alleviated in the 1970s. Anyoha (2017) submits that between 1957 and 1974 AI flourished. Computers could store more information and they became faster, cheaper and more accessible. The prerequisite for intelligence was now met, hence the flourishing of AI.

Haenlein and Kaplan (2019) concur with the points above. They point to the development of the expert systems such as ELIZA and the General Problem Solver as one of the first major developments. There were still challenges though, as Haenlein and Kaplan (2019) point out, that both ELIZA and the General Problem Solver were based on the expert systems, which is 'the collections of rules which assume that human intelligence can be formalized and reconstructed in a top-down approach as a series of "if-then" statements'.

2.4 What Is AI? Some Definitions of AI

Tran et al. (2019), Kirsh (1991), Allen (1998), Hearst and Hirsh (2000), Brachman (2006), Nilsson (2009), Bhatnagar et al. (2018) and Monett and Lewis (2018) have all indicated that the term artificial intelligence has no universally agreed definition. Examined literature indicates that definitions of AI have changed over time as technology develops. As a result, different entities have defined AI based on their focus. Wang (2019) concurs that there is no fixed definition for AI primarily because of intelligence complexity. This complexity makes it unrealistic to expect a commonly accepted definition of AI.

According to Haenlein and Kaplan (2019), AI can be defined as 'the system's ability to interpret external data correctly, to learn from such data, and to use those learnings to achieve specific goals and tasks through flexible adaptation'. According to Marr (2018), AI refers to 'the theory and development of computer systems that are able to perform tasks that normally require human intelligence'. Examples of the tasks include visual perception, speech recognition, decision-making and translation between languages (Marr, 2018).

According to Copeland (2020), AI refers to 'the ability of a digital computer or computer–controlled robot to perform tasks that are commonly associated with intelligent human beings'. This involves the development of systems that are equipped with intellectual processes that characterise humans. Examples of these intellectual processes include ability to reason, discover meaning, learn from experience or generalise (Copeland, 2020).

Merriam-Webster (2018) defines AI as 'the field of computer science that is committed to solving intellectual problems that are analogous to human intelligence such as learning, problem solving, and pattern recognition. This field of science deals with the simulation of cognitive behaviour in computers'. Noyes (2016) defines AI as 'an extensive collection of methods, algorithms and technologies that make software intelligent in a way that seem human-like to an observer'.

From so many definitions of AI, Faggela (2018) comes up with what he calls an informed definition of AI. It states that AI is an entity that is capable of receiving inputs from the environment and then interpret and learn from those inputs, the associated evidence and flexible behaviours and actions that assist the entity to realise a specific goal over a course of time.

Each of the definitions given above addresses a particular aspect of AI, thus confirming that there is no universally accepted definition to date. What we are learning from these definitions is that AI is centred on the ability of machines to imitate human intellectual behaviour, e.g. the imitation of human intellectual behaviour by computer systems.

2.5 Weak and Strong AI

The concepts of weak and strong AI emanate from Searle's (1980) objection to the argument put forward by the proponents of the idea that the relation between the brain and the body of a human being is identical in many respects to the relation between the hardware and the software of AI and machine consciousness (MC). In attacking this idea, Searle (1997) points to the fact that the 'implemented program, by itself could be viewed as constitutive of having a mind'. In addition, Searle (1997) points out that the implemented program guarantees mental life.

Searle (1980) argues that there are two categories, namely, weak AI and strong AI. For Searle (1980), strong AI can be thought of as a process of seeking to produce a mind or an intelligence. This mind will possess and understand other mental states. Accordingly, the developed machine could be said to have a mind, though this mind will be grounded on programs which run on hardware. This, accordingly, is the opposite of the mind that emerges from biology.

Furthermore, Searle (1980) views the weak AI as 'an attempt at modelling the human mind in a similar way to modelling weather conditions, climate change, or other natural phenomena. By extension, weak AI does not aim to reproduce, or produce a mind any more than a computer model of an ongoing storm seeks to reproduce an actual storm'.

According to Puaschunder (2019), weak AI describes the situation where the computer is solely an instrument that investigates intellectual processes. According to IBM (2021), weak AI could be characterised by specific tasks. An example of this would be a machine that is trained to answer specific questions. From this example, what is clear is that this machine performs one task. The reliance of weak AI is on human intervention. Human beings will define the parameters for the machine learning algorithms. Furthermore, humans will provide the training data to feed into the machine.

Puaschunder (2019) defines AI as the computer processes that are intellectual and self-capable to achieve the learning processes. IBM (2021) indicates that the strong AI could be characterised by machines' ability to perform a variety of functions. The machine will also be eventually capable of teaching itself to solve new problems. Here lies the difference: in weak AI, the reliance is on human interference to define the parameters, whereas in strong AI the machine is capable of learning.

Wisskirchen et al. (2017) further expatiate on these categories of AI and state that weak AI is labelled as artificial narrow intelligence (ANI), while strong AI is further split between artificial general intelligence (AGI) and artificial super intelligence (ASI).

2.6 Some Developments of the Key AI Technologies Today

AI research is an ever-evolving field since it came to the fore in the 1940s. According to Bonasio (2020), in recent times, AI research has grown by 12.9% annually worldwide. Bonasio (2020) paints the following global developments regarding AI:

- In the next 4 years, there are predictions that China will become the biggest global source of AI.
- China will be followed by the United States.
- India is seen as the third largest country in terms of AI research.
- This will be followed by Europe. Accordingly, Europe is the largest and most diverse region with high levels on international collaboration within the field of AI research (Bonasio, 2020).

Edureka (2020) and Advani (2019) have identified the top 15 AI technologies that are in the spotlight today. These are the natural language generation (NLG), the natural language understanding (NLU), speech recognition (SR), ML, virtual agents (VL), expert systems (ES), decision management (DM), deep learning (DL), robotic process automation (RPA), text analytics (TA), natural language processing (NLP), biometrics, cyber defence (CD), emotion recognition (ER) and image recognition (IR).

Since AI technologies are rapidly changing due to demand, the list of technologies constantly changes. Detailed discussion of each technology is provided below.

2.6.1 Natural Language Generation (NLG)

NLG is a sub-discipline of AI that converts text into data. It conveys a message by predicting the next word in a sentence. It further assists in the communication of ideas and thoughts in a clear manner. NLG uses language models which are probability distribution over sequences of words, to predict which likely word among millions of possibilities is targeted. As a procedure, its aim is to transform any structured data into a natural language. Put in simple terms, NLG can be thought of as a process that converts thoughts into words. The NLG is widely employed in customer service to create reports and market summaries (Advani, 2019; Edureka, 2020).

2.6.2 Natural Language Understanding (NLU)

As will become clearer in the discussions below, the NLU is the polar opposite of NLG. Whereas the NLG uses AI to convert text into data, NLU uses computer software to interpret text and certain types of unstructured data. According to Gartner (2019), NLU can be thought of as the comprehension of the structure and meaning of human language by computer programs. This allows users to interact with the computer using natural sentences. Therefore, this technology can digest a text, translate it into computer language and produce an output in a language that humans can understand (Advani, 2019; Edureka, 2020).

2.6.3 Speech Recognition (SR)

Typically, SR uses AI to convert and transform human speech into a useful and comprehensive format for computer applications to process. AI algorithms are designed in a way that allows them to understand human speech in several natural languages. The AI technology further enables the algorithm to have a faster and smoother interaction with humans. SR is seen as a bridge in human-computer interaction (Advani, 2019; Edureka, 2020).

2.6.4 Machine Learning (ML) Platforms

Machine learning platforms concentrate on training a computer to learn and think on its own. If it does this, then it passes the Turing test and can be deemed intelligent. ML would normally employ intricate algorithms for training the computer. Typically, during the training, the computer is given a set of classified and unclassified training data related to either a specific or a general domain.

The machine would analyse this data and then draw inferences. It continues to store this data for future use. In future, when the machine encounters any other sample data of the domain that it would have already learned, it goes to its mental compartments where the stored data is to draw inferences, reach necessary conclusions and give an appropriate response.

2.6.5 Virtual Agents (VA)

VA can be thought of as an exhibition of a technology which aims to create an effective but digital impersonation of humans. Accordingly, this technology uses the combination of AI programming, ML and NLP among other forms to understand the customer and their grievances. This is the reason the VA is a prominent technology in the customer care industry. Examples of VA are Chatbots and smart home managers. As technology advances, what is becoming clear is that these systems are getting better in interacting with humans in a humane way (Advani, 2019; Edureka, 2020).

2.6.6 Expert Systems (ES)

ES in AI are computer programs that use pre-stored knowledge base. The pre-stored knowledge base is used to mimic the decision-making ability of humans. These systems employ reasoning ability and the predefined 'if-then' type of rules. Accordingly, these types of systems are highly efficient in solving complex problems (Advani, 2019; Edureka, 2020).

2.6.7 Decision Management (DM)

DM systems highly rely on AI's abilities to interpret and convert customer data into predictive models of key trends. In the long run, these models enable firms to take necessary and effective decisions. These DM applications provide automated decision-making capabilities.

Most firms deploy the DM systems in marketing and consumer departments. They are pivotal in customising the departmental efforts according to key data required by these departments. Accordingly, the development of commercial AI in decision management systems is focused on three particular sectors, namely, e-commerce, financial markets and insurance (Advani, 2019; Edureka, 2020).

2.6.8 Deep Learning (DL) Platforms

DL is thought of as a special subset of ML based on artificial neural networks (ANN). DL duplicates the neural circuits of the human brain to process data and create patterns for decision-making. Accordingly, learning is carried out at different levels where each level is capable of transforming the input dataset into composite and abstract representations.

The term "deep" refers to the number of levels of data transformation carried out by the computer system. Some of its applications are automated speech recognition, image recognition and prediction of anything that can be sensed in the digital sphere (Advani, 2019; Edureka, 2020).

2.6.9 Robotic Process Automation (RPA)

RPA refers to the functioning of the firm's processes as a result of mimicking human tasks and automating them. RPA involves mechanical, computer-controlled devices to perform tasks that require extreme precision or tedious or hazardous work by people.

RPA is used mostly in industrial levels to automate various processes. Such automated systems help in larger domains where it is not feasible to employ humans. However, while manual robotics is capable of completing jobs, it often lacks the necessary automation required to complete the task without human intervention (Advani, 2019; Edureka, 2020).

2.6.10 Text Analytics (TA)

TA is defined as an analysis of text structure. Typically, it uses TA to interpret and learn the structure, meaning and intentions of any particular text they may come across. In most cases, the TA system has been applied in security and fraud detection systems.

Since an AI-enabled system has the ability to distinguish between any two types of text samples without any human intervention, it is then deemed independent. It is this independence that enables such a system to be effective, efficient and faster than its human counterparts (Advani, 2019; Edureka, 2020).

2.6.11 Natural Language Processing (NLP)

NLP's main focus is on the interactions between human languages and computers. The NLP uses TA to analyse the structure of sentences. It also uses TA to analyse interpretation and intention through ML. The NLP technology is widely adopted in fraud detection and in security systems. Accordingly, most automated assistants and applications derive unstructured data from NLP (Advani, 2019; Edureka, 2020).

2.6.12 Biometrics

The biometrics AI technology deals with the recognition, measurement and analysis of the physical features of the body's structure, form and human behaviour. The biometrics AI technology fosters organic interactions between machines and humans. It typically works with touch, image, speech and body language (Advani, 2019; Edureka, 2020).

2.6.13 Cyber Defence (CD)

The cyber defence technology is a computer defence mechanism that aims to detect, prevent and mitigate attacks and threats to data and ICT infrastructure. Typically, the neural networks (NN) that are capable of processing sequences of inputs can be put to use along with ML techniques to create learning technologies in order to reveal suspicious user activity and detect cyber threats (Advani, 2019; Edureka, 2020).

2.6.14 Emotion Recognition (ER)

The ER technology enables emotions expressed by humans to be read and interpreted using advanced image processing or audio data processing. The ER technology is often employed in law enforcement activities (Advani, 2019; Edureka, 2020).

2.6.15 Image Recognition (IR)

IR could be viewed as a 'process of identifying and detecting an object in a digital image, and one of the uses of computer vision'. It can also be called image classification. The technology can help the process of image searches greatly as well as detect licence plates, diagnose diseases and study personalities (Advani, 2019; Edureka, 2020).

2.7 Key Points

- Historically, AI came into the spotlight driven by allies on the two sides of the Atlantic Ocean, namely, the United Kingdom and the United States.
- Turing put together and published *Computing Machinery and Intelligence*, which became a seminal work.
- This treatise brought with it the Turing test. The Turing test can be explained as follows: if a human is interacting with a machine, but he/she is unable determine whether he/she is interacting with a machine or a human being, then that machine is viewed as intelligent.
- In the United States, the concept of AI was inspired by science fiction known as *Runaround* created by Isaac Asimov.
- The DSRPAI was an important convention which propelled AI a step forward.

- There were major challenges in AI as early computers could not store commands. They only executed them. Another early challenge in the computing world was that computers were unaffordable.
- Various definitions of AI exist. Examined literature indicates that definitions of AI have changed over time as technology develops.
- Different entities have defined AI based on their focus.
- There is weak and strong AI. The concept of weak and strong AI emanates from Searle's (1980) objection to the argument put forward by the proponents of the idea that the relation between the brain and the body of a human being is identical in many respects to the relation between the hardware and the software of AI and MC.
- Weak AI is characterised by a machine performing specific tasks.
- Strong AI is characterised by the machine's ability to perform a variety of functions. The machine will also be eventually capable of teaching itself to solve new problems.
- In the strong AI, the developed machine could be said to have a mind; however, this mind will be grounded on programs which run on hardware.
- There is a variety of AI technologies that are in the spotlight today, namely, the NLG, NLU, SR, ML, VA, ES, DM, DL, RPA, TA, NLP, biometrics, CD, ER and IR.
- As technology advances, expectations are that technologies in spotlight will also progress to keep tabs with time.

References

Advani, V. (2019). *Top 10 hot artificial intelligence (AI) technologies*. Available from https://www.mygreatlearning.com/blog/top-10-hot-artificial-intelligence-technologies/

Allen, J. F. (1998). AI growing up: The changes and opportunities. *AI Magazine, 19*(4), 13–23.

Anyoha, R. (2017). *The history of artificial intelligence: Can machine think?* Available at https://sitn.hms.harvard.edu/flash/2017/history-artificial-intelligence/

Bhatnagar, S., Alexandrova, A., Avin, S., Cave, S., Cheke, L., Crosby, M., Feyereisl, J., Halina, M., Loe, B. S., hEigeartaigh, S. O., Martnez-Plumed, F., Price, H., Shevlin, H., Weller, A., Winfield, A., & Hernandez-Orallo, J. (2018). Mapping intelligence: Requirements and possibilities. In V. C. Muller (Ed.), *Philosophy and theory of artificial intelligence 2017* (pp. 117–135). Berlin: Springer.

Bonasio, A. (2020). *Report: Global AI research*. Available at https://techtrends.tech/tech-trends/report-global-ai-research/

Brachman, R. J. (2006). (AA)AI – more than the sum of its parts, 2005 AAAI presidential address. *AI Magazine, 27*(4), 19–34.

Copeland, B. J. (2020). *What is artificial intelligence?* Available from http://www.alanturing.net/turing_archive/pages/Reference%20Articles/What%20is%20AI.html

EDUREKA. (2020). *Top 15 hot artificial intelligence technologies*. Available from: https://www.edureka.co/blog/top-15-hot-artificial-intelligence-technologies/

Faggela, D. (2018). *Artificial intelligence industry – an overview by segment*. Available from: https://www.techemergence.com/artificial-intelligence-industry-an-overview-by-segment/vs-ai-industry/

GARTNER. (2019). *Hype cycle for artificial intelligence*. Accessed March 19, 2020, from https://www.gartner.com/en/documents/3953603/hype-cycle-for-artificial-intelligence-2019

Haenlein, M., & Kaplan, A. (2019). A brief history of artificial intelligence: On the past, present, and future of artificial intelligence. *California Management Review, 61*(4), 5–14.

Hearst, M. A., & Hirsh, H. (2000). AI's greatest trends and controversies. *IEEE Intelligent Systems*, 8–17.

IBM. (2021). *Weak vs. strong AI*. Available at https://www.ibm.com/cloud/learn/strong-ai#:~:text=Weak%20AI%2C%20also%20known%20as,to%20solve%20for%20new%20problems

Kirsh, D. (1991). Foundations of AI: The big issues. *Artificial Intelligence, 47*, 3–30.

Marr, B. (2018). *The key definitions of artificial intelligence (AI) that explain its importance*. Available from https://www.forbes.com/sites/bernardmarr/2018/02/14/the-key-definitions-of-artificial-intelligence-ai-that-explain-its-importance/

Merriam-Webster. (2018). *The key definitions of artificial intelligence (AI) that explain its importance*. Available from https://www.forbes.com/sites/bernardmarr/2018/02/14/the-key-definitions-of-artificial-intelligence-ai-that-explain-its-importance/

Monett, D., & Lewis, C. W. P. (2018). Getting clarity by defining artificial intelligence – A survey. In V. C. Muller (Ed.), *Philosophy and theory of artificial intelligence 2017* (pp. 212–214). Berlin: Springer.

Nilsson, N. J. (2009). *The quest for artificial intelligence: A history of ideas and achievements*. Cambridge: Cambridge University Press.

Noyes, K. (2016, March 3). *5 Things you need to know about A.I.: Cognitive, neural and deep, oh my!* Computerworld. Retrieved at www.computerworld.com/article/3040563/enterprise-applications/5-things-you-need-toknow-about-ai-cognitive-neural-anddeep-oh-my.html

Puaschunder, J. M. (2019). Artificial intelligence evolution: On the virtue of killing in the artificial age. *Journal of Sociology, 3*(1), 10–29.

Searle, J. R. (1980). Minds, brains and programs. *Behavioral and Brain Sciences, 3*, 417–457.

Searle, J. R. (1997). *The mystery of consciousness*. London: Granta Books.

Smarzo, B. (2017). *Isaac Asimov: The 4th law of robotics*. Available at https://infocus.delltechnologies.com/william_schmarzo/the-4th-law-of-robotic-artificial-intelligence/

Turing, A. (1950). Computing Machinery and Intelligence. *Mind, LIX/236*, 433–460.

Tran, B. X., Laktin, C. A., Sharafeldin, N., Nguyen, K., Vu, G. T., Tam, W. W. S., Cheung, N., Nguyen, H. L. T., Ho, C. S. H., & Ho, R. C. M. (2019). Characterizing artificial intelligence applications in cancer research: a latent dirichlet allocation analysis. *JMIR Medical Informatics, 7*(4), e14401.

Wang, P. (2019). On defining artificial intelligence. *Journal of Artificial General Intelligence, 10* (2), 1–37. https://doi.org/10.2478/jagi-2019-0002.

Wisskirchen, G., Biacabe, B. T., Bormann, U., Muntz, A., Niehaus, G., Soler, G. T., & Brauchtsch, B. (2017). *Artificial intelligence and robotics and their impact on the workplace*. IBA Global Employment Institute.

A Brief Overview of the Firm's Strategy

3

3.1 Introduction

Chapter 2 introduced AI. A high-level overview of AI was provided. It discussed the early days of AI. This discussion was followed by a discussion of significant developments in AI following the early slow start. Chapter 2 further provided some definitions of AI. What was evident in the discussion of definitions is that there is no standard definition of AI. It then discussed the differences between weak and strong AI. Finally, it outlined the current developments and discussed some of the key modern-day AI technologies.

Strategy as a concept emanates from the need of the people to defeat their adversaries. Horwath (2020) points out that strategy can be traced back to the period between 200 B.C. and 400 B.C. Both Horwath (2006) and Syed (2014) trace the first text that emphasised strategy to *The Art of War*, which was written by Sun Tzu between 400 B.C. and 500 B.C.

This chapter provides a high-level overview of strategy by discussing the historical account of strategy in Sect. 3.2. This is followed by a discussion in Sect. 3.3 that is aimed at understanding the concept of strategy. Section 3.4 provides a generic overview of strategy definitions, and Sect. 3.5 outlines and discusses processes that firms ought to engage in as they formulate strategy.

3.2 A Brief History of Strategy Origination

The first text around the strategy appeared around 400 B.C. written by Sun Tzu. Syed (2014) indicates that this book remains the most widely read book in military history. From the firm's perspective, one of the ideas often used is that of winning a battle without fighting. Accordingly, firm hierarchy has often thought of this as the best way to win. The term strategy itself is said to emanate from the Greek word 'strategos'. According to Horwath (2020), 'strategos simply means "general"'. It is

T. Moloi, T. Marwala, *Artificial Intelligence and the Changing Nature of Corporations*, Future of Business and Finance,
https://doi.org/10.1007/978-3-030-76313-8_3

derived from the Classic and Byzantine which came into light around 330 A.D. (Horwath, 2020).

According to Horwath (2006), the history of strategy can be traced back to the need of people to defeat their adversaries. Henderson (1989) concurs with this statement. This is clear in his articulation of strategy where he indicates that competition existed long before the word strategy was coined. As such, competition began with life itself. Seen from the perspective of life, Henderson (1989) points out that to maintain life, a one-cell organism required certain resources.

Adequate resources guarantee that the organism can grow the next generation of other organisms. Accordingly, as life evolves, the organisms also evolve to become 'a resource for a more complex source of life'. As it happens when life evolves, different pairs of organisms emerge and begin to compete for the resources. This leads to displacement of one organism by the other. The absence of the counter-balancing mechanism necessary to maintain a stable equilibrium, so that each organism has advantage over a certain territory, causes a displacement of the weaker organism. In Henderson's (1989) words, 'only one of any pairs survived'.

Mintzberg and Quinn (1991) have put forward an argument that strategy was already considered as a key organisational process by the time of Pericles (450 B.C.). According to Mainardes et al. (2014), this means that management skills such as administrative, leadership, public speaking and power were already considered then. However, Mainardes et al. (2014), citing Bracker (1980), note that 'it was only after World War II that strategy fully entered into the business world. Strategy has grown significantly since the war'.

3.3 Understanding Strategy: An Overview

Strategy refers to a way in which companies explain to their stakeholders how they will be moving forward. The question is answered in a broader form rather than specifics, i.e. it is less specific than the plan of action. According to Nagy and Fawcett (n.d.), good strategies take into account barriers and resources at the disposal of a firm. Furthermore, a good strategy will also stay with the overall vision, mission and the stated objectives.

The firm strategy is generally viewed as a course of action that can help the firm in attaining its objectives (Furrer, 2013). In other words, firm strategy is viewed as a master plan that the leadership of a firm implement to get a competitive position in the market, which will allow it to satisfy customers and at the end be able to attain its desired goals (Furrer, 2013; Rennison et al., 2014). This view is consistent with Nagy and Fawcett (n.d.).

According to Furrer (2013) and Rennison et al. (2014), firm strategy is implemented to fulfil the objectives set by the policy of the firm. As the leaders of a firm craft strategy, they should always be cognisant of the objectives of a firm and think of the ways in which a firm can build a competitive strategy in a particular market or business. For Yang et al. (2015), firm strategy can be described as a 'way in which a company creates value through a successful coordination of its different activities'.

In concurring with the above, Chandler (1962) proposes that the strategy defines 'long-term goals and objectives of a firm, the adoptions of actions, and the allocation of necessary resources for the achievement of the objectives'. Andrews (1971) views the strategy as 'the model of the objectives, policies, purposes, goals, and plans that the firm intends to achieve'.

One of the minds that have been cited widely when it comes to the concept of strategy is Porter. According to Porter (2008), strategy entails the selection of 'the set of activities in which a firm stands out to establish a sustainable difference in the market'. When it comes to the differentiation, Porter has submitted that it arises from the activities chosen and from how these are carried out.

In view of this, Yang et al. (2015) define firm strategy differently to Furrer (2013) and Rennison et al. (2014). Accordingly, the strategy can be viewed as 'a plan for the generation of economic profits premised on lower cost, better quality, and even new products' (Yang et al., 2015).

The most critical building block in firm strategy is the issue of resources because these determine what a firm can do (Hendry & Kiel, 2004). Resources also give direction to the business pertaining to the nature of business the firm should concentrate on and which can give it competitive advantage (Hendry & Kiel, 2004). When the business shares resources across related businesses, it achieves economies of scale, synergies and corporate advantage (Jacobs & de Man, 1996). The ability of a business to have mobile resources provides the firm with an advantage to diversify and to give diversification strategy to the firm (Lechner & Gudmundsson, 2014).

3.4 Some Definitions of Strategy

The discussions below present various definitions of strategy. These were sourced from Mainardes et al. (2014).

The 1940s and the 1950s saw two definitions of strategy emerge. First, strategy was viewed as a series of actions undertaken by a firm, based on a particular situation (Von Neumann & Morgenstern, 1947). Then, for Drucker (1954), strategy involves the process of analysing the present situation and then responding to the outcome of the analysis by changing the situation, should the analysis dictate.

In the 1960s, Chandler (1962) argued that strategy could be viewed as the determinant of the basic long-term goals of a firm. Furthermore, it speaks to the adoption of courses of action and the allocation of resources necessary for carrying out these goals. Ansoff (1965) views strategy as a rule for making decisions. These decisions are the result of the firm's interaction with its environment when it comes to the product/market scope, growth vector, competitive advantage and synergy.

Cannon (1968) proposes that strategy should be seen in the context of the directional action decisions which are competitively required to achieve the firm's purpose, whereas Learned et al. (1969) indicate that strategy refers to the pattern of objectives, purposes or goals and major policies and plans by a firm with the aim being to achieve the objectives.

The early 1970s saw some additional definitions emerging. Newman and Logan (1971) emphasise that strategies can be thought of as forward-looking plans that assist a firm to anticipate changes and then move to initiate action so as 'to take advantage of opportunities that are integrated into the concepts or mission of the firm'. For Schendel and Hatten (1972), strategy should be understood as the basic goals and objectives of the firm. Accordingly, strategy speaks to 'the major programs of action chosen to reach these goals and objectives, and the major pattern of resource allocation used to relate the firm to its environment'.

The mid-1970s saw Uyterhoeven et al. (1973) indicating that a strategy will consist of several steps such as formulating the 'strategic profile, strategic forecast, resource audit, strategic alternatives explored, tests or consistency and, finally, strategic choice'. Ackoff (1974) indicates that strategy can be thought of as deliberate effort 'concerned with long-range objectives and ways of pursuing them that affect the system as a whole'. For Paine and Naumes (1975), a strategy contains some 'macro-actions or patterns of actions for achieving the objectives of the company'.

In the view of McCarthy et al. (1975), the term strategy refers to the 'analysis of the environment where the firm is located and the selection of alternatives that will direct the resources and objectives of the firm, taking into consideration the risk and potential profits, and the feasibility that each alternative offers'. For Glueck (1976), a strategy should be seen as a 'unified, comprehensive, and integrated plan designed to assure that the basic objectives of the enterprise are achieved'. Michel (1976) argues that a strategy should involve decisions and allocation of resources to 'take advantage of opportunities and minimise factors that threaten the achievement of desired results'.

In the late 1970s, other definitions of strategy emerged. For example, McNichols (1977) indicates that a strategy should be a process that is 'embedded into policy-making'. Typically, a strategy will contain 'a series of decisions that reflect the basic objectives of the firm's business, and how to use the capabilities and internal resources to achieve these objectives' (McNichols, 1977). For Steiner and Miner (1977), strategy is supposed to be seen a process. This process deals with the formulation of a 'mission, purposes and basic firm goals, policies and programs to meet them, and the methods needed to ensure that strategies are implemented to achieve firm's objectives'.

At the end of the 1970s, Ansoff (1979) reviewed the 1960s definition. In the new definition, strategy could be viewed as a 'set of rules for decision making under conditions of partial ignorance'. The aspect of the ecosystem was retained in the new definition. In this regard, Ansoff (1979) indicates that strategic decisions concern the firm's relationship with its ecosystem. In addition, Mintzberg (1979) views strategy as an important aspect of a firm as it plays a 'mediating force between the firm and its environment: consistent patterns in streams of firm's decisions to deal with the environment'.

3.5 Strategy Formulation

According to Satyro et al. (2017), the strategy formulation process has a positive effect on process innovation performance, product innovation performance and marketing innovation performance. In concurring with Satyro et al. (2017), Nwachukwu et al. (2018) indicate that systematic strategy formulation processes are important, especially when firms want to attain process innovation and performance.

According to Satyro et al. (2017), even though there are benefits to the use of adequate strategy to reach competitive advantage, most firms pay very little attention to understanding the strategy formulation process for environmental sustainability.

For Oyedele et al. (2019), strategy adoption on its own is not enough, but the strategy should be followed up to the point of implementation and control to ensure that it will have desired outcomes for the firm. Furthermore, Oyedele et al. (2019) advise that strategy formulation, adoption and implementation have power to determine the profitability and efficiency of a firm, as strategies that are formulated and implemented will have a greater influence on the market share of the firm.

Oyedele's view is shared by Borrero et al. (2020). They explored how strategy formulation affects the performance of the firm, with a deep desire to assess whether rational/analytical strategy formulation is more effective than reflexive strategy formulation. The study discovered that the formal strategy formulation process is related to firm performance. Borrero et al. (2020) also found out that rational approaches are more effective than emergent/reflexive approaches in improving firm performance, especially for cultures with a low future orientation.

Strategy formulation is defined as 'a process undertaken to determine and establish the goals, mission, and objectives of a firm' (Saylor, 2013). During the process of strategy formulation, the firm can identify the appropriate and best courses of action from all the available strategies that can be used to achieve them (Saylor, 2013). Furthermore, strategy formulation could be viewed as a 'process undertaken where a firm will choose the most appropriate course of action to attain its defined goals' (Saylor, 2013).

The above views are consistent with those of Cannon (1968) and Collis and Montgomery (2005) who indicate that the strategy formulation process is 'a purposeful, linear, sequential and deliberate exercise to realise the firm's vision and mission'. Accordingly, strategy formulation is crucial to the success of the firm because it gives the firm a framework for the actions that will result in the attainment of the anticipated results (Binladen & Al-Ashaab, 2017; Dayan et al., 2017).

A framework for the success of the firm is achieved through analysing and understanding the influential factors that affect the firm in its ecosystem (Davidson et al., 2015) and influence the firm's ability to observe, monitor and assimilate those factors (Bilgili et al., 2016). Another critical component in strategy formulation is that it should be communicated to everyone in the firm so that they become aware of the firm's objectives, mission and purpose (Binladen & Al-Ashaab, 2017; Yang et al., 2015).

The NGOBG (2001) describes mission as the 'agreed-upon statement by the firm and it explains the reason for its existence. Accordingly, the mission is necessarily broad so that it can encompass the diversity within the firm. It is important to note that the mission statement is not precise in its measurements nor does it need to be, but it does need to be periodically reviewed'. When it comes to the objective, the NGOBG (2001) describes it as 'the areas of emphasis, rather than specific statements with a specific goal'.

Saylor (2013) posits that strategy formulation acts as a force for the firm to change the environment and to be well prepared for any possible changes that may happen. In this regard, strategy formulation is crucial in assisting a firm to make some evaluations on the resources which will assist in budget allocation, as well as in the determination of the most effective plan for maximising return on investment (Lambaerts, 2017; Pitt & Treen, 2017).

For Bordean et al. (2010), strategy formulation is important because a firm that does not take time to do proper strategy formulation will not be able to plan or properly guide its employees and give them focus. Furthermore, a firm that does not have a strategic plan will not have a perfect competitive advantage because the firm will be reactive to business conditions rather than being proactive in addressing unanticipated challenges.

In the view of Klettner et al. (2014), large businesses should have at least two strategies, namely, the corporate-level strategy and the business-level strategy. These are briefly outlined below:

- The corporate-level strategy—The corporate strategy should focus more on the identity of the firm, the vision, the purpose, goals, portfolio investments, policies for controlling subsidiaries and business-level objectives (Bartholmé & Melewar, 2016; Leong & Jarmoszko, 2010). Steyn and Niemann (2010) concur with Bartholmé and Melewar (2016) and Leong and Jarmoszko (2010) that corporate strategy represents the highest level of strategy, at which ideas can be formulated and where policies can be deployed.
- The business-level strategy—The business-level strategy is usually positioned between the upper management and the front-level operations (Agarwal & Ansell, 2016). It is more localised and it deals with the activities of each functional area, as well as how each functional area can maximise resource allocation (Mitchell, 2009; Wooldridge & Floyd, 1990).

According to Andrews (1999) and Drnevich and Croson (2013), strategy development should focus more on decision-making and deployment, which include prioritisation and allocation of resources for profit and future market position. It has also been highlighted that corporate-level strategy usually takes a proactive position in strategy formulation, while business-level strategy takes a reactive position. The other important aspect of corporate and business strategy is that corporate strategy mainly focuses on actively seeking and analysing the external environment continuously, while business mainly focuses on the delivery of products and services effectively and efficiently.

Fig. 3.1 Three aspects of strategy formulation. Source: Authors own illustration

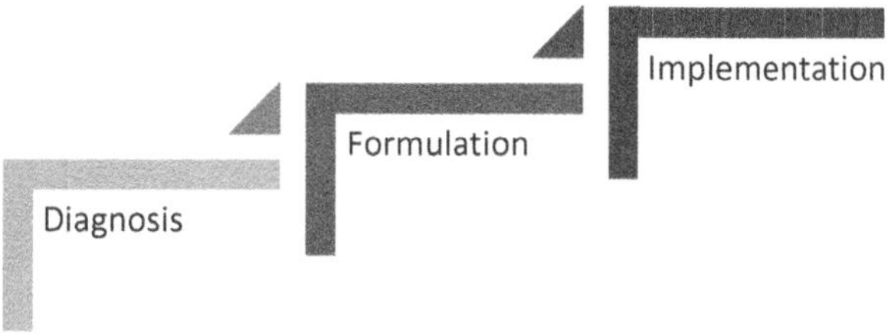

Fig. 3.2 Three phases of strategy formulation. Source: Authors own illustration

According to Mitchell (2009), there are three aspects of strategy formulation. These aspects are corporate-level strategy, the competitive strategy (sometimes called the business strategy) and the parenting strategy (Fig. 3.1).

The levels of strategy have different focus areas, and they should therefore be dealt with accordingly in the formulation phase (Nwachukwu et al., 2018). Corporate-level strategy focuses more on the broad decisions of the firm's scope and direction. The business will consider any changes that can be made on the growth objective and all the available strategies to attain it. It also investigates all the lines of business, specifically how these lines fit together. The corporate-level strategy has three main components, namely:

- The growth or directional strategy, which outlines the growth objective of the firm and mainly on how to achieve this
- The portfolio strategy, which outlines the portfolio of the lines of the firm, which assist in the diversification that the business should engage in
- The parenting strategy that explains how resources are allocated and managed, especially on areas on which to put more emphasis

According to Mitchell (2009), it is important to take strategy formulation as part of the broader management process that includes three phases, which are the diagnosis, formulation and implementation (Fig. 3.2).

3.6 Diagnosis

Accordingly, strategic management and formulation should be taken as an ongoing process that is critical in developing and revising future-oriented strategies that will help the firm to attain its objectives, to consider its capabilities, constraints and the environment in which it operates. Diagnosis further involves carrying out a situation analysis where the internal environment of the firm is analysed, which includes the proper identification and valuation of the current mission, strategic objectives, strategies and the results, including major strength and weaknesses (Mitchell, 2009).

Diagnosis also involves the analysis of the firm's external environment, which comprises the opportunities and threats (Mitchell, 2009; Pitt & Treen, 2017). Lastly, diagnosis involves the identification of the critical issues, which are normally viewed as a small set. Typically, this includes two to five of the firm's major problems, threats, weaknesses and opportunities that demand high priority and attention (Mitchell, 2009).

3.7 Formulation and Implementation

According to Mitchell (2009), strategy formulation is taken as the second phase in the strategic management process which produces recommendations that are clear and support justifications which can revise as necessary the mission and objectives of the firm and give strategies for attaining them. It was also revealed that in strategy formulation, the current objectives of the firm are modified in ways that make the firm successful.

These actions involve the creation of sustainable and competitive advantages, which can be eroded by the actions of competitors. In the implementation process, the recommendations should be effective enough to solve the stated problems and can be implemented with the available resources, should be feasible within the period, must be cost-effective, are not overly disruptive and should be acceptable by key stakeholders in the firm.

Different authors and those who adopted the formal approach in the strategy formulation process have interpreted strategy formulation process differently. Lambaerts (2017) and Wheelen and Hunger (2012) propose internal and external scanning where the vision, mission and objectives are defined, followed by corporate strategy, and then the functional strategy is implemented.

For Sminia (2009), Pearce and Robinson (2011), Andrews (1999) and Thaha (2015), steps in strategy formulation involve defining the vision, mission and objectives and analysing the environment. After this process, Sminia (2009), Pearce and Robinson (2011), Andrews (1999) and Thaha (2015) propose the firm should develop the firm strategy and then the functional strategy.

Lambaerts (2017) disagrees with strategy formulation as proposed by the above scholars. Lambaerts (2017) laments that:

- This approach may not be useful in unstable economies.
- It lacks (has no built-in process) a process that provides feedback from customers and stakeholders.
- The approach is rigid. It could just as well pose difficulties in making the firm adaptive.

However, Lambaerts (2017) concedes that in a stable environment, such an approach is helpful especially for new product development and even for instituting new changes to the internal environment. According to Saylor (2013), strategy formulation requires six steps for it to be effective. These are:

- Defining the firm—This is related to identifying the company's customers. The main reason for identifying these customers is to make sure that the firm identifies the major factors that these customers value. This will enable the company to identify the needs of the company relative to what the competitors are offering. The firm should answer the question of whether the customers buy the product from the firm due to its price or whether the products are meeting the needs of the customers (Ivančić et al., 2018; Kolosova & Sidorov, 2018).
- Defining the strategic mission—The strategic mission of firm offers a long-term perspective of the aims of the firm going forward. Accordingly, the mission statement helps the firm to carry out its plans successfully (Budiman et al., 2020). The mission is also required to contain strong elements of the values that the firm holds, the nature of the business, the market power of the firm and the vision of the firm.
- Defining the strategic objectives—The formulation of strategic objectives demands that the firm identify performance targets required to attain the objectives of the firm. Some objectives can be 'market position relative to the competition, production of goods and services, desired market share, improved customer services, corporation expansion, advances in technology, and sales increases' (Saylor, 2013).

  The other critical point is to ensure that these objectives are communicated to everyone in the firm so that the success of the firm is guaranteed. Furthermore, all members of the firm should know the role they play in the firm and the magnitude of their contributions towards the attainment of the firm's objectives (Borrero et al., 2020).
- Defining the competitive strategy—The competitive strategy of the firm is crucial to see where the firm fits in the broader market (Saylor, 2013). Competitive strategy applies to the entire firm. It also applies to the individual units and departments (Kolosova & Sidorov, 2018; Saylor, 2013). Each unit in the firm must be aware of its role and of how that role influences the competitive position of the firm. The other important aspect is the development of proactive responses to anticipated changes in the market (Saylor, 2013). As highlighted earlier, a firm should not wait for marketplace events to happen before taking the necessary steps, but it should identify potential events and be prepared to act. The final and important step for competitive strategy formulation is identifying the resources of the firm to determine how properly they should be used (Saylor, 2013). Each division of the firm will have a set of needs; therefore, the firm must be able to determine how these resources are allocated to satisfy those needs (Saylor, 2013; Zerfass & Viertmann, 2017).
- Implementing strategies—The final output of the strategy formulation process is the configuration of business activities, resources and operations to attain the

corporate vision and mission. In the traditional or convectional approach (this is sometimes referred to as the prescriptive approach or design school of thought), strategy formulation is led by the top management team and the process is a centralised and rational decision-making led the process (Lambaerts, 2017). The process of disseminating the strategy of the business starts at the central corporate level and then moves to the business level (Mintzberg & Waters, 1985; Lambaerts, 2017).

- Evaluating progress—This is the final step following the execution of the strategy.

3.8 Key Points

- Strategy as a concept emanated from the need of the people to defeat their adversaries.
- The concept of strategy can be traced back to the period between 200 B.C. and 400 B.C.
- The first text that emphasised strategy was *The Art of War*, which was written by Sun Tzu sometime between 400 B.C. and 500 B.C.
- From a business perspective, strategy refers to a way in which firms explain to their stakeholders how they will be moving forward.
- Firm strategy is generally viewed as a course of action that can help the firm in attaining its objectives.
- There are three aspects of strategy formulation, namely, the corporate-level strategy, the competitive strategy (sometimes called the business strategy) and the parenting strategy.
- The growth or directional strategy outlines the growth objective of the firm and mainly on how to achieve this.
- The portfolio strategy outlines the portfolio lines of the firm, which assist in the diversification that the business should engage in.
- The parenting strategy explains how resources are allocated and managed; it pays special attention to areas that require more emphasis.
- Strategy contains three phases, and these are diagnosis, formulation and implementation phases.

References

Ackoff, R. (1974). *Redesigning the future*. New York: Wiley. isbn:04-7100-296-8.

Agarwal, R., & Ansell, J. (2016). Strategic change in enterprise risk management. *Briefings in Entrepreneural Finance*. https://doi.org/10.1002/jsc.2072.

Andrews, K. R. (1971). *Concept of corporate strategy*. Homewood, IL: Irwin.

Andrews, K. R. (1999). *The concept of corporate strategy*. New York, NY: Primis Custom Pub.

Ansoff, H. (1965). *Corporate strategy: An analytic approach to business policy for growth and expansion*. New York: McGraw-Hill. ISBN 00-7002-111-2.

Ansoff, H. (1979). *Strategic management*. London: Macmillian. ISBN 04-7026-585-X.

Bartholmé, R. H., & Melewar, T. C. (2016). The end of silence? Qualitative findings on corporate auditory identity from the UK. *Journal of Marketing Communications, 22*(4), 419–436. (Abingdon: Taylor & Francis, ISSN 1352-7266, ZDB-ID 1317851-9).

Bilgili, B., Özkulb, E., & Candan, B. (2016). An outlook on "all inclusive" system as a product diversification strategy in terms of consumer attitudes. *12th international strategic management conference, ISMC 2016,* 28–30 October 2016, Antalya, Turkey.

Binladen, H., & Al-Ashaab, A. 2017. *Strategy formulation process in large family-based businesses*. Available at http://www.iaras.org/iaras/journals/ijems

Bordean, O. N., Borza, A., Rus, C., Bordean, O., Borza, A., Rus, C. and Mitra, C. 2010. *An investigation on the strategy formulation process within the Romanian companies*. Available at https://www.researchgate.net/publication/254392092

Borrero, S., Acosta, A., & Medina, A. F. (2020). Culture, strategy formulation, and firm performance: A meta-analysis. *Academia Revista Latinoamericana de Administracion, 33*(1), 147–176. https://doi.org/10.1108/ARLA-01-2018-0013.

Bracker, J. (1980). The historical development of the strategic management concept. *Academy of Management Review, 5*(1), 219–224. ISSN 0363-7425.

Budiman, Y., Amar, M., Sanusi, A., & Ariesca Riana, M. (2020). Strategy formulation for performance improvement of the artificial insemination program in Sinjai regency. *IOP Conference Series: Earth and Environmental Science, 575*(1), 012233. https://doi.org/10.1088/1755-1315/575/1/012233.

Cannon, J. (1968). *Business strategy and policy*. New York: Harcourt, Brace & World. ISBN 65-4317-252-0.

Chandler, A. (1962). *Strategy and structure: Chapters in the history of the American industrial enterprise*. Cambridge: MIT Press. ISBN 15-8798-198-X.

Collis, D., & Montgomery, C. (2005). *Corporate strategy: A resource-based approach*. Boston, MA: Irwin McGraw-Hill.

Davidson, S., Harmer, M., & Marshall, A. (2015). Strategies for creating and capturing value in the emerging ecosystem economy. *Strategy and Leadership, 43*(2), 2–10. https://doi.org/10.1108/SL-01-2015-0003.

Dayan, R., Heisig, P., & Matos, F. (2017). Knowledge management as a factor for the formulation and implementation of organization strategy. *Journal of Knowledge Management, 21*(2), 308–329. https://doi.org/10.1108/JKM-02-2016-0068.

Drnevich, P. L., & Croson, D. C. (2013). Information technology and business level strategy. *MIS Quarterly, 37*(2), 483–509.

Drucker, P. (1954). *The practice of management*. New York: Harper & Brothers. ISBN 00-6091316-9.

Furrer, O. (2013). *Business policy and corporate strategy*. Available at https://www.researchgate.net/publication/236694166

Glueck, W. (1976). *Business policy, strategy formation, and management action* (2nd ed.). New York: McGraw-Hill. ISBN 00-7023-514-7.

Henderson, B. D. (1989). The origins of strategy. *Harvard Business Review*. Available at https://hbr.org/1989/11/the-origin-of-strategy?registration=success

Hendry, K., & Kiel, G. C. (2004). The role of the board in firm strategy: Integrating agency and organisational control perspectives. *Corporate Governance: An International Review, 12*(4), 500–520. https://doi.org/10.1111/j.1467-8683.2004.00390.x.

Horwath, R. (2006). *The origin of strategy*. Strategic Thinking Institute. Available at https://www.strategyskills.com/Articles/Documents/origin_strategy.pdf

Horwath, R. (2020). *The origin of strategy*. Strategic Thinking Institute. Available at https://www.strategyskills.com/the-origin-of-strategy/#:~:text=The%20term%20%E2%80%9Cstrategy%E2%80%9D%20is%20derived,Greek%20ever%20used%20the%20word.&text=Igor%20Ansoff%20(Corporate%20Strategy%2C%201965,to%20give%20it%20a%20name

Ivančić, V., Jelenc, L., & Mencer, I. (2018). *The strategy formulation – Implementation relationship and the leaders role during the implementation process*.

Jacobs, D., & de Man, A. P. (1996). Clusters, industrial policy and firm strategy: A menu approach. *Technology Analysis and Strategic Management, 8*(4), 425–438. https://doi.org/10.1080/09537329608522461.

Klettner, A., Clarke, T., & Boersma, M. (2014). The governance of corporate sustainability: Empirical insights into the development, leadership and implementation of responsible business strategy. *Journal of Business Ethics, 122*, 145–165. https://doi.org/10.1007/s10551-013-1750-y.

Kolosova, I. I., & Sidorov, I. V. (2018). Principles of Formation of Filling Station Spatial Environment Abroad. Vestnik Tomskogo Gosudarstvennogo Arkhitekturno-Stroitel'nogo Universiteta. *Journal of Construction and Architecture, 2*, 61–75. https://doi.org/10.31675/1607-1859-2018-20-2-61-75.

Lambaerts, P. (2017) *The strategy formulation practices of a newly appointed top management team.* Masters Thesis, JAMK University of Applied Sciences. Available at https://core.ac.uk/download/pdf/84799083.pdf

Learned, E., Christensen, R., Andrews, K., & Guth, W. (1969). *Business policy: Text and cases.* Homewood, IL: Irwin. ISBN 76-1459-813-0.

Lechner, C., & Gudmundsson, S. V. (2014). Entrepreneurial orientation, firm strategy and small firm performance. *International Small Business Journal: Researching Entrepreneurship, 32*(1), 36–60. https://doi.org/10.1177/0266242612455034.

Leong, L., & Jarmoszko, A. (2010). Analyzing capabilities and enterprise strategy: A value proposition framework. *International Journal of Management & Information Systems (IJMIS), 14*(1), 53–60.

Mainardes, E.W.; Ferreira, J.J. and Raposo, M.L. 2014. *Strategy and strategic management concepts: Are they recognised by management students.* Ekonomika a Management. Available at http://legado.fucape.br/_public/producao_cientifica/2/Strategy%20And%20Strategic.pdf

McCarthy, D., Minichiello, R., & Curran, J. (1975). *Business policy and strategy: Concepts and readings.* Homewood, IL: Irwin. ISBN 02-5601-680-1.

McNichols, T. (1977). *Policy making and executive action* (5th ed.). New York: McGraw-Hill. ISBN 00-7045-688-7.

Michel, K. (1976). Design of an intrafirm management development programme for strategic managers. In H. Ansoff, R. Declerck, & R. Hayes (Eds.), *From strategic planning to strategic management* (pp. 152–171). London: Wiley. ISBN 04-7103-223-9.

Mintzberg, H. (1979). *The structuring of organizations.* Englewood Cliffs, NJ: Prentice-Hall. ISBN 01-3855-270-3.

Mintzberg, H., & Quinn, J. (1991). *The strategy process: Concepts, contexts and cases* (2nd ed.). Englewood Cliffs, NJ: Prentice-Hall. ISBN 01-3851-916-1.

Mintzberg, H., & Waters, J. (1985). Of strategies, deliberate and emergent. *Strategic Management Journal, 6*(3), 257–272.

Mitchell, R. C. 2009. *Strategy formulation.* Available at: https://resources.saylor.org/wwwresources/archived/site/wp-content/uploads/2013/04/BUS300-2.3_Strategy-Formulation.pdf

Nagy, J., & Fawcett, S. B. (n.d.). *Chapter 8: Section 4. Developing successful strategies: Planning to win.* Available at https://ctb.ku.edu/en/table-of-contents/structure/strategic-planning/develop-strategies/main

Newman, W., & Logan, J. (1971). *Strategy, policy and central management.* Cincinnati: South-Western Publishing. ISBN 00-2072-409-0.

NGOBG. (2001). *Strategic planning handbook.* Available at https://www.ngobg.info/bg/documents/49/753sphand.pdf

Nwachukwu, C., Chladkova, H., & Fadeyi, O. (2018). Strategy formulation process and innovation performance nexus. *International Journal for Quality Research, 12*(1), 147–164. https://doi.org/10.18421/IJQR12.01-09.

Oyedele, A. F., Sotunde, O. A., Oyedele, O. O., Oladokun, O. O., Makinde, K. O., & Fabinu, B. T. (2019). The relationship of strategy formulation, adoption, and implementation to small scale market share performance. *The Pacific Journal of Science and Technology, 20*(2), 141. http://www.akamaiuniversity.us/PJST.htm.

Paine, F., & Naumes, W. (1975). *Strategy and policy formation: An integrative approach.* Philadelphia: Saunders. ISBN 47-2938-411-0.

Pearce, J. A., & Robinson, R. B. (2011). *Strategic management: Formulation, implementation and control.* New York: McGraw Hill.

Pitt, C. S., & Treen, E. (2017). Understanding communication in disaster response: A marketing strategy formulation and implementation perspective. *Journal of Public Affairs, 17*(3), e1639. https://doi.org/10.1002/pa.1639.

Porter, M. (2008). *Competitive advantage: Creating and sustaining superior performance.* New York, NY: Simon and Schuster.

Rennison, L., Novin, F., & Verstraete, M. (2014). Firm strategy, competitiveness and productivity: The case of Canada. Available at https://www.bankofcanada.ca/wp-content/uploads/2014/11/boc-review-autumn14-rennison.pdf

Satyro, W. C., Sacomano, J. B., Contador, J. C., Almeida, C. M. V. B., & Giannetti, B. F. (2017). Process of strategy formulation for sustainable environmental development: Basic model. *Journal of Cleaner Production, 166*, 1295–1304. https://doi.org/10.1016/j.jclepro.2017.08.128.

Saylor, O. (2013). *The Saylor Foundation.* Available at: www.saylor.org/bus208

Schendel, D., & Hatten, K. (1972). Business policy or strategic management. In Mitchell, V., Barth, R., & Mitchell, F. (Eds.). *Academy of management proceedings* (pp. 56–72). Boston: Little Brown. ISSN 0896-7911.

Sminia, H. (2009). Process research in strategy formation: Theory, methodology and relevance. *International Journal of Management Reviews, 11*(1), 97–125.

Steiner, G., & Miner, J. (1977). *Management policy and strategy: Text, readings and cases.* New York: Macmillan. ISBN 00-2416-750-9.

Steyn, B., & Niemann, L. (2010). Enterprise strategy: A concept that explicates corporate communication's strategic contribution at the macro-organisational level. *Journal of Communication Management, 14*(2), 106–126. https://doi.org/10.1108/13632541011034574.

Syed, M. (2014). *Brazil's buckling revealed dark side of human psyche.* Available at https://www.thetimes.co.uk/article/brazils-buckling-revealed-dark-side-of-human-psyche-fm3hqgx62gq

Thaha, A. R. (2015). *Business strategy formulation and implementation for CETAKBDG.* Available at https://www.researchgate.net/publication/328118116_BUSINESS_STRATEGY_FORMULATION_AND_IMPLEMENTATION_FOR_CETAKBDG

Uyterhoeven, H., Ackerman, R., & Rosenblum, J. (1973). *Strategy and organization: Text and cases in general management.* Homewood, IL: Irwin. ISBN 02-5601-923-1.

Von Neumann, J., & Morgenstern, O. (1947). *Theory of games and economic behaviour* (2nd ed.). Princeton: Princeton University Press. ISBN 06-9100-362-9.

Wheelen, T. L., & Hunger, J. D. (2012). *Strategic management and business policy: Toward global sustainability* (13th ed.). Upper Saddle River, NJ: Pearson Prentice Hall.

Wooldridge, B., & Floyd, S. W. (1990). The strategy process, middle management involvement, and organizational performance. *Strategic Management Journal, 11*, 231–241.

Yang, M. J., Kueng, L., & Hong, B. (2015). *Business strategy and the management of firms.* NBER Working Paper. Available at http://www.nber.org/papers/w20846

Zerfass, A., & Viertmann, C. (2017). Creating business value through corporate communication: A theory-based framework and its practical application. *Journal of Communication Management, 21*(1), 68–81. https://doi.org/10.1108/JCOM-07-2016-0059.

Strategy Implementation 4

4.1 Introduction

Chapter 3 provided a high-level overview of strategy. It discussed the historical account of the strategy, followed by a discussion aimed at exploring the concept of the strategy. It further outlined and discussed processes that firms ought to engage in as they formulate strategy. From the discussions, it became apparent that strategy has long existed within living organisms. Strategy as a concept emanated from the need of the people to defeat their adversaries.

From the discussions in Chap. 3, it has become clear that strategic management is a crucial activity in a firm's life. It was also made apparent in the discussions that a strategic session is crucial as it is used to formulate the firm's sets of decisions, actions and measures. These sets are subsequently implemented to achieve the firm's goals and objectives.

At a broader level, the strategy contains three phases, namely, diagnosis, formulation and implementation. An overview of both the strategy diagnosis and formulation was briefly presented in Chap. 3. Chapter 4 briefly discusses strategy implementation.

The rest of the chapter is organised as follows: Sect. 4.2 provides some definitions of strategy implementation, followed by a brief distinction between strategy implementation and strategy execution in Sect. 4.3. Section 4.4 briefly outlines some activities in strategy implementation, whereas Sect. 4.5 provides some factors that firms need to consider as they implement strategies. Section 4.6 outlines the typical pitfalls and mitigations for successful strategy implementation.

T. Moloi, T. Marwala, *Artificial Intelligence and the Changing Nature of Corporations*, Future of Business and Finance,
https://doi.org/10.1007/978-3-030-76313-8_4

4.2 Some Definitions of Strategy Implementation

According to the Chartered Management Institute (2014), strategy implementation is defined as 'the way an firm should develop, utilize, and amalgamate firm structure, control systems, and culture to follow strategies that lead to competitive advantage and a better performance'.

Giles (1991) views the strategy implementation as the execution of tactics so that the firm moves in the desired strategic direction. According to Noble (1999a, 1999b), strategy implementation is a 'relatively straightforward operationalisation of a clearly articulated strategic plan'. For Wheelen and Hunger (2006), strategy implementation refers to 'the sum of the total activities and choices required for the execution of a strategic plan'.

Since the term strategy refers to long-term planning, the implementation part is executed to ensure that the firm's long-term goals are achieved (Hrebiniak, 2006). Strategy implementation is also viewed as a technique through which the firm develops new processes that are subsequently utilised and integrated into the firm's structure (Obeidat et al., 2017; Olson et al., 2018; Tawse & Tabesh, 2021).

4.3 Strategy Implementation vs Execution

In Favaro's view, strategy implementation and strategy execution are two different things. However, Belyh (2020) argues that these terms are used interchangeably. According to Belyh (2020), strategy implementation refers to a step where a firm translates its chosen strategy into action, plans and activities.

Favaro (2015) seems to agree that the implementation involves the translation of the firm's chosen strategy into action, plans and activities. However, in Favaro's view, the firm's strategy execution occurs when the firm puts the plans in motion and performs the activities.

The Chartered Management Institute (2014) and Obeidat et al. (2017) do not differentiate between strategy implementation and execution. Accordingly, strategy implementation is seen as a process where a firm translates its chosen strategy into action plans and activities (Chartered Management Institute, 2014; Obeidat et al., 2017).

The action plans and activities aim to help the firm to achieve its strategic objectives (Chartered Management Institute, 2014; Hrebiniak, 2006; Okumus, 2001). Thus, in the view of the Chartered Management Institute (2014), Hrebiniak (2006) and Okumus (2001), the process of strategy implementation can be viewed as the process of executing plans outlined in the strategy.

Similar to the submission by the Chartered Management Institute (2014) and Obeidat et al. (2017), Miller (2020) describes strategy implementation as 'the process of turning plans into action to reach a desired outcome'. Miller (2020) refers to this as 'the art of getting stuff done'. Without getting 'the stuff done', the firm will not be successful. This view is consistent with Hrebiniak's (2005) argument that senior-level executives will always be 'faced with the straightforward task of simply getting things done'. In other words, the success of every firm rests on its capacity to implement decisions and execute key processes efficiently, effectively and consistently (Miller, 2020).

4.4 An Overview of Activities in Strategy Implementation

According to Belyh (2020), there are five primary activities in strategy implementation. They include the following:

- The establishment of the firm's annual objectives
- The formulation of policies for the execution of the firm's strategies
- The plan around the allocation of resources
- The actual performance of the stated tasks and activities
- The process of leading and controlling the actual performance of activities or tactics at various levels of the firm

According to Cater and Pucko (2010), there are four activities in strategy implementation, and these are planning activities, organising activities, leadership activities and controlling activities. A brief description of each activity is captured below:

- Planning activities—Planning a firm's activities involves programming and budgeting (Puko, 2006) and developing programmes, budgets and procedures (Wheelen & Hunger, 2006). It also involves translating strategy into projects (Pellegrinelli & Bowman, 1994) and managing projects (Grundy, 1998; Hauc & Kova, 2000; Kova, 1996; Minarro-Viseras et al., 2005; Puko, 2006). Furthermore, planning the activities also involves establishing operating-level objectives (Hrebiniak & Joyce, 1984), tactical (annual) planning (Puko, 2006) and annual business planning (Birnbaum, 2007). Finally, it involves action planning (Birnbaum, 2007; Puko, 2006; Wheelen & Hunger, 2006) and turning strategy into action (Farsight Leadership Organisation, 2007).
- Organising activities—This involves fitting the organisation to the strategy: organisation design (Kova, 1996; Lorange, 1982), designing primary and operating organisational structures (Hrebiniak & Joyce, 1984), organising for strategy implementation (Puko, 2006), organising for action (Wheelen & Hunger, 2006) and developing organisational structure (Birnbaum, 2007). It further involves translating enterprise-level plans into lower unit-level plans (Kaplan & Norton, 2005), allocating responsibility for strategy implementation (Puko, 2006) and involving people from all organisational levels (Wheelen & Hunger, 2006).
- Leadership activities—Leadership activities involve triggering enthusiasm in employees (Nicholls, 1994), giving them direction (Puko, 2006), leading by coaching people (Wheelen & Hunger, 2006), being motivational leaders (Farsight Leadership Organisation, 2007) and leading the change (Brenes et al., 2008). They further include emphasising communication between all parties

(Al-Ghamdi, 1998), communicating the corporate strategy to the entire firm (Kaplan & Norton, 2005) and communicating strategy to people outside the firm (Speculand, 2006). Furthermore, they include aligning employees' goals with strategic goals (Kaplan & Norton, 2005) and managing through objectives (Puko, 2006; Wheelen & Hunger, 2006). In addition to the above, leadership activities include executing human resources activities (Fulmer, 1990; Ulrich, 1998), staffing (Puko, 2006; Wheelen & Hunger, 2006) and managing human resource factors (Birnbaum, 2007).
- Controlling activities—The controlling activities involve the creation of incentives and control mechanisms (Hrebiniak & Joyce, 1984), the controlling of the implementation of strategies (Puko, 2006), monitoring and control (Birnbaum, 2007) and implementing control and follow-up actions (Brenes et al., 2008). It further involves using the balanced scorecard (Kaplan & Norton, 1996, 2006) and consistently measuring progress and performance (Farsight Leadership Organisation, 2007).

4.5 Considerations for Successful Strategy Implementation

Favaro (2015) concurs that strategy consists of corporate strategy and business unit strategy. These two categories have been discussed in detail in Chap. 3 of this book. In explaining corporate strategy, Favaro (2015) indicates that this is a session by senior executives of a firm. In this session, senior executives are most concerned about three questions, and these are:

- What should be the capabilities that distinguish the firm from its competitors?
- What should be the firm's comparative advantage in adding value to its businesses (including segments)?
- What businesses should the firm be involved in to ensure that it is successful? (Favaro, 2015)

As senior executives of a firm make choices on capabilities that distinguish the firm, identifying their niche market (comparative advantage) and making a choice on the line of business, they also need to make decisions around their target market, the value proposition of their product and infrastructure that will make a firm better in delivering the value proposition (Favaro, 2015). In this regard, the firms' senior executives would ask the following questions in order to make critical decisions:

- Who should be the customers that define a firm's target market?
- What should be the value proposition that differentiates the firm's products and services from those of competitors?
- What should be the capabilities that make the firm better than any of its competitors in delivering the value proposition? (Favaro, 2015)

Simons (2010) concurs that firm executives should ask themselves serious questions about their strategy. This is because 'successful business strategy lies not in having all the right answers, but rather in asking the right questions'. Simons (2010) proposes seven questions in this regard, namely:

- Who are the firm's primary customers? Here, Simons (2010) argues that the most critical strategic decision for any business is determining clients to which it seeks to provide a product. If this is done, Simons (2010) believes, it could permit the business to devote all possible resources to meeting their needs and minimising resources devoted to everything else. Accordingly, Simons (2010) is of the view that this is the path to competitive success.
- How do the firm's core values prioritise vital stakeholders such as shareholders, employees and customers? When it comes to this question, Simons (2010) advises that firms need to define their core values to prioritise the key stakeholders. This is important because it indicates whose interest comes first when faced with difficult trade-offs.
- What critical performance variables does the firm track? Simons (2010) advises that firms should set the right goals, assign accountability and monitor performance to deliver on the strategic imperatives successfully.
- What are the strategic boundaries that the firm has set for itself? Since every strategy brings the risk that an individual's actions will pull the business off course, Simons (2010) advises that firms set strategic boundaries to control the strategic risks.
- How is the firm generating creative tension? Simons (2010) advises that firm's executives should encourage and reward innovation. This is important because the competition will likely decimate firms that fail to innovate.
- How committed are the firm's employees to helping each other? Innovation provides an opportunity for the employees to compete with each other. If this occurs, employees are unlikely to collaborate, which could have an impact on the firm's strategy.
- What strategic uncertainties keep the firm's executives awake at night? Adapting to change is critical to the survival of a firm. As such, executives must set up a firm to be agile to survive the booms and busts, the changing customer preferences, the behaviour of competitors (e.g. introduction of new products) and the emerging disruptive new technologies.

According to Belyh (2020), five factors are crucial to strategy implementation. They include people, resources, structure, systems and culture. Brief explanations of these are given below:

- People—As firms consider strategy, they should check if they have a sufficient workforce to deliver on the strategic imperative. More than a question of numbers, this becomes a question of the right people with the right skill sets.

- Resources—As a firm considers strategy, it has to allocate adequate resources to provide support to the business units to execute the strategy. Resources include human capital, time and financial resources.
- Structure—As a firm considers strategy, the executive layer of the firm must define the lines of communication throughout the firm. Furthermore, Belyh (2020) suggests that employees, even those on the lowest tier of the firm hierarchy, must communicate with their supervisors and top management and vice versa. Ensuring an open and transparent communication network will facilitate the implementation process. Belyh (2020) submits that the firm's structure must be properly laid out. In addition to this, it is recommended that the firm ensures that each of its members knows the person they are accountable to and who they are responsible for.
- Systems—As a firm considers strategy, the executive layer of the firm must ask itself several questions on:
  - The systems, tools and capabilities that the firm has in place to facilitate the implementation of the strategies
  - The specific functions of these systems
  - How these systems will aid the firm in the succeeding steps of the strategic management process following their implementation (Belyh, 2020)
- Culture—As a firm considers strategy, the executive layer of the firm must gauge the overall atmosphere within the firm. Belyh (2020) argues that to successfully implement its strategy, a firm will need to promote a culture of being responsible and accountable (responsibility and accountability). Furthermore, a firm must create a sanction and a reward system that corresponds with excellent and poor performance. Accordingly, this can create an atmosphere where everyone within a firm is motivated to contribute to the implementation of strategies.

4.6 Pitfalls and Mitigations in Strategy Implementation

4.6.1 Pitfalls in Strategy Implementation

The Chartered Management Institute (2014) advises that the success of any chosen strategy depends on its implementation. As the strategy is formulated, it is essential that it does not become a simple expression of hopes and aspirations for the future. Instead, it should consist of practical implications for the operations of the firm, which should be thought through and put into practice.

To successfully implement strategy, it is essential that firms formulate initiatives that are focused and reliable (Lahkar & Mukherjee, 2020; Tawse & Tabesh, 2021). Tawse and Tabesh (2021) indicate that strategic failures experienced by many firms emanate from the inability of the senior leadership team to ensure that firm strategy consists of practical implications for the operations of the firm.

Other challenges that lead to a firm failing to implement its strategy may include:

- Weak or inconsistent senior-level commitment
- Lack of support from managers and employees
- Cross-departmental conflicts
- Ambiguity in roles and responsibilities or a lack of accountability (Lahkar & Mukherjee, 2020; Tawse & Tabesh, 2021; the Chartered Management Institute, 2014)

4.6.2 Mitigations in Strategy Implementation

Bakero and Maina (2020), Köseoglu et al. (2020) and Olson, Slater, and Hult (2005) indicate that there are various critical steps that need to be taken into consideration for the senior leadership of a firm to understand the complexities of the implementation of a strategy, for instance. These critical steps give guidance on the factors that can assist the firm to attain optimal, rather than the maximal, implementation of a strategy (Köseoglu et al., 2020; Olson et al., 2005). These steps include:

- Ensuring that plans are well aligned to the firm's mission, vision and values (Chartered Management Institute, 2014; Olson et al., 2005). This step ensures that the implementation of plans is premised on the objectives and strategy of the firm (Noble, 1999a, 1999b; Olson et al., 2005).
- Building an effective leadership team (Olson et al. 2005). This step is critical because optimal implementation of a strategy is premised on professionalism, especially management and leadership capacity of the strategic and operational managers (Chartered Management Institute, 2014; Lemarleni et al., 2017). Lemarleni et al. (2017) add that it is also important for leaders to adjust their leadership styles and the learning management techniques and approaches. Adjustment of leadership style is important because strategy implementation can alter priorities, change resource allocation and even shift relationships, which can pose threats to the power and status of some influential people within the firm (Fedato et al., 2017). For Lindsay et al. (2018), it is important to build the right team for the success of strategy execution, and firms should have the mechanism for recruitment of the right people required. Senior members and the human resource department should join hands in the recruitment of the team (Fedato et al., 2017; Lindsay et al., 2018).
- Formulating the implementation plan (Lindsay et al., 2018; Mailu et al., 2018). The full implementation plan should be created for the firm and, more importantly, for all the levels of the firm (Lindsay et al., 2018). The implementation plan should state the resources required and the steps needed to attain the objectives (Noble, 1999a, 1999b; Olson et al., 2005). The financial resources, personnel and operational and technological resources required should be quantified, and the plan should identify the people responsible for individual initiatives (Cadwallader et al., 2010; Elbanna & Fadol, 2016). The implementation plan assists in setting priorities, accountabilities and the short-term and long-term objectives of the firm (Atkinson, 2006; Bourgeois & Brodwin, 1984).

Personal accountabilities are critical in the implementation plan so that individuals understand their responsibilities (Fedato et al., 2017; Mailu et al., 2018). Atkinson (2006) argues that the strategic implementation plan should be drafted in a way that makes it simple to be articulated into separate action plans for each project and initiative, and the project implementation process and project management practices should be adhered to. The implementation plan should also be visible so that it does not become disconnected from the decision-making process and it should be accessible to everyone (Amoo et al., 2019; Andrews et al., 2011; Atkinson, 2006).

- Allocation of budgetary resources (Lemarleni et al., 2017). Securing enough budget is one of the critical elements of the implementation of a strategy (Lemarleni et al., 2017). According to Olson et al. (2005), when a firm formulates a strategy, this process could put additional demand for financial resources in order to develop new processes, for purchase of new equipment and even for the recruitment of new employees among other initiatives. As a result, budgetary support is required to ensure that all these initiatives are properly resourced and can be implemented at the right time. For this to take place, Olson et al. (2005) and Mailu et al. (2018) have argued that the budgetary process needs to be aligned with the strategy. In addition, both the operating and capital budgets need to be linked with each aspect of strategy (Mailu et al., 2018).
- Assigning objectives and responsibilities (Abujarad, 2020). According to Abujarad (2020), strategic responsibilities and objectives should be assigned clearly to enable employees to better understand their roles and responsibilities within the strategy. If this is done properly, individuals are likely to take ownership of specific strategic tasks and outcomes (Abujarad, 2020; Chartered Management Institute, 2014). Everyone assigned a role to play in the implementation needs to have a clear idea of the outcomes and the responsibility they hold for these outcomes to be fulfilled (Andrade-Rochin & Gustavo, 2020). The duty to ensure that all the employees understand the roles they play and how their roles contribute to the objectives of the firm rests with the senior leadership team as it formulates and monitors strategy implementation (Andrade-Rochin & Gustavo, 2020). According to Andrade-Rochin and Gustavo (2020), it is better to assign the objectives and responsibilities to individuals rather than to teams. As these are assigned, they should be explicit so that clear personal accountability is maintained. Elbanna and Fadol (2016) concur with this view, and they further indicate that for proper implementation of a strategy, employees at all levels should be aware of how their performance is measured and evaluated. Furthermore, Elbanna and Fadol (2016) state that metrics for all the tasks should be created to enable the individuals to know the intended outcomes and the expected time frames. In the situation where strategic objectives and outcomes are not measured, it is very difficult to hold individuals to account (Atkinson, 2006; Bourgeois & Brodwin, 1984). Andrade-Rochin and Gustavo (2020) warn that while some outcomes like profit growth are relatively easy to record and measure, some important aspects to this, like staff morale and engagement, require softer metrics.

- Alignment of structures and processes (Andrade-Rochin & Gustavo, 2020). In strategy implementation, alignment of structures and processes should be a priority. In most cases, the plans, processes and structures of many firms operate in isolation and often with little relationship even to the firm's strategy (Elbanna & Fadol, 2016). For a firm to be able to implement strategy effectively, structures and processes need to be aligned with the strategic objectives (Bryson & Bromiley, 1993; Cadwallader et al., 2010). In the alignment of the structure of the firm to strategic objectives, activities should be coordinated, and the skills and capabilities of the firm should be made available for the benefit of the firm (Elbanna & Fadol, 2016). In addition, it is important to align the ongoing and proposed projects to strategic objectives (Piórkowska & Ryńca, 2020). A full assessment and evaluation of the contribution of each project towards the strategic objectives will inform decisions such as which projects should be resourced and carried through to completion (Andrade-Rochin & Gustavo, 2020).
- Alignment of human capital (Chartered Management Institute, 2014). This is one of the effective tools in strategy implementation. Bryson and Bromiley (1993) posit that effective people management is an important issue in the successful implementation of a strategy. The contributions of all the firm's employees should be aligned with the strategy of the firm (Mailu et al., 2018). This alignment helps employees to align with the achievement of the firm's objectives (Mailu et al., 2018). The behaviour that is required in the firm and the cultural issues should also be defined (Mailu et al., 2018; Tawse & Tabesh, 2021). Lindsay et al. (2018) argue that for the implementation to be successful, it is important that firms create a cohesive strategy that employees can understand and effectively engage with. The knowledge that they are contributing to the firm is very important to employees (Lindsay et al., 2018).
- Communication of strategy across the firm (Mailu et al., 2018). Communication of strategic imperatives is another critical aspect of strategy implementation. All critical stakeholders, particularly the firm's employees, should understand the core elements of the strategy and the way this strategy should be executed. According to Köseoglu et al. (2020), this is a critical component for encouraging employee buy-in, commitment and engagement. Köseoglu et al. (2020) also argue that communication of the strategy normally has a positive impact on productivity. In order to ensure that people understand the firm's strategy, vague statements should be avoided, and objectives should be expressed concretely and measurably with results that are tangibly achievable in expected time frames (Köseoglu et al., 2020). The Chartered Management Institute (2014) outlines important issues to be considered in communicating strategy, namely, the messages to be communicated, audience to be reached, behavioural changes needed, communication channels to be used and measures to evaluate the level of success or failure. According to Lahkar and Mukherjee (2020), merely handing a copy of the strategy is rarely effective. As such, there should be a separate document that must be prepared with a summary of critical and significant points which are clear and concise. The other mistake that should be avoided is jargon,

as the message should be simple, clear, convincing and compelling (Lahkar & Mukherjee, 2020).

- Reviewing and reporting progress is another important aspect of strategy implementation (Tawse & Tabesh, 2021). Reviewing progress should be done regularly to check if the strategy is being implemented as planned (Tawse & Tabesh, 2021). This stage is critical because managers can track progress, check on priorities and identify any issues that may require tackling (Bakero & Maina, 2020). Strategy review has more to do with results than control on performance (Bakero & Maina, 2020). Meetings to review the strategy should be done continuously to keep the implementation process on course and to allow the managers to take decisions on any required adjustments (Bakero & Maina, 2020). Reviews can be weekly at first, then bi-weekly, then monthly and then quarterly. The frequency of the reviews needs to be scaled back especially when the implementation process has been established and the managers are sure that it is now working very well (Bakero & Maina, 2020). The frequency of the meetings also depends on the activities undertaken. Sometimes more frequency is required when the strategy is coming up with major changes to the firm and when the business environment is evolving rapidly (Bakero & Maina, 2020).
- Strategy adjustments (Tawse & Tabesh, 2021). Where necessary, strategic adjustments should be taken very seriously in the strategy implementation process. Adjustments are necessary because strategy implementation takes place in an environment where there are economic, social and competitive circumstances in which changes are ever present (Olson et al., 2018). Leadership skills and capabilities are measured in this phase (Olson et al., 2018).
- The development of a firm culture that will provide support to the strategy (Okumus, 2001). Firm culture plays a critical role in translating strategic plans and initiatives into action. Despite how good the strategy is, the implementation of the strategy will be affected should it not be supported by the firm's culture (Hrebiniak, 2006). Hrebiniak (2006) argues that a culture that is well aligned to the firm's strategy will assist the firm to implement strategy well, as there would be a shared belief in the firm's aims and objectives.

Given these mitigations, it is apparent that in strategy implementation, the senior leadership should avoid taking strategy implementation as a simple process, being taken by surprise when unanticipated market changes occur and require adjustments; managers should avoid committing insufficient resources to support the successful execution of the strategy (Pitt & Treen, 2017). It is also important that managers avoid failure in aligning the firm's design and capabilities with the strategy (Nwachukwu et al., 2018). The other important aspect is that managers should avoid failure to communicate the strategy consistently and persistently within the firm. Lastly, managers should avoid bureaucratic and time-consuming processes in strategy implementation and reporting, which can consume important time that should be used for real issues (Satyro et al., 2017).

4.7 Key Points

- To successfully implement strategy, the senior leadership team within a firm must ensure that plans are well aligned to the firm's mission, vision and values.
- The optimal implementation of a strategy is premised on professionals, especially management and leadership capacity of the strategic and operational managers.
- It is also important for leaders to adjust their leadership styles as well as learning management techniques and approaches. Adjustment of leadership style is important because strategy implementation can alter priorities, change resource allocation and even shift relationships, which can pose threats to the power and status of some influential people within the firm.
- The full implementation plan should be created for the firm and more importantly for all the levels of the firm.
- The financial resources, personnel and operational and technological resources required should be quantified, and the plan should also identify the people responsible for individual initiatives.
- Securing enough budget is one of the critical elements of the implementation of strategy.
- Strategic responsibilities and objectives should be assigned clearly to enable employees to understand their roles and responsibilities within the strategy.
- In strategy implementation, alignment of structures and processes should be a priority. In most cases, many firms' plans, processes and structures operate in isolation and sometimes with little relationship even to the firm strategy.
- It is important to align the ongoing and proposed projects to strategic objectives.
- It is essential to align the human capital to the strategy. Effective people management is an essential issue in the successful implementation of a strategy.
- All critical stakeholders, particularly the firm's employees, should understand the core elements of strategy and the way this strategy should be executed.
- Reviewing progress in achieving the strategic imperatives should be done regularly to check if the strategy is being implemented as planned.
- Where necessary, strategic adjustments should be taken very seriously in the strategy implementation process. Adjustments are necessary because strategy implementation occurs in an environment where there are unique economic, social and competitive circumstances.
- A firm's culture plays a critical role in translating strategic plans and initiatives into action.
- The senior leadership team should avoid taking strategy implementation as a simple process, as they will be surprised when unanticipated market changes occur.
- The firm's senior leadership should avoid committing insufficient resources to support the successful execution of strategy.

References

Abujarad, A. H. A. (2020). *The effect of leadership styles on strategy implementation in NGOs: A case study of Gaza strip View project*. https://doi.org/10.13140/RG.2.2.14469.17121.

Al-Ghamdi, S. M. (1998). Obstacles to the successful implementation of strategic decisions: The British experience. *European Business Review, 98*(6), 322–327.

Amoo, N., Hiddlestone-Mumford, J., Ruzibuka, J., & Akwei, C. (2019). Conceptualizing and measuring strategy implementation: A multidimensional view. *Strategic Change, 28*(6), 445–467. https://doi.org/10.1002/jsc.2298.

Andrade-Rochin, & Gustavo, A. (2020). *Durham E-theses lean strategy implementation challenges*. http://etheses.dur.ac.uk/13783/http://etheses.dur.ac.uk

Andrews, R., Boyne, G. A., Law, J., & Walker, R. M. (2011). Strategy implementation and public service performance. *Administration and Society, 43*(6), 643–671. https://doi.org/10.1177/0095399711412730.

Atkinson, H. (2006). Strategy implementation: A role for the balanced scorecard? *Management Decision, 44*(10), 1441–1460. https://doi.org/10.1108/00251740610715740.

Bakero, H. S., & Maina, R. (2020). Strategy implementation and performance of tana river county government. *Journal of Strategic Management, 4*(1), 16–34. https://stratfordjournals.org/journals/index.php/journal-of-strategic-management/article/view/456.

Belyh, A. (2020). *Essential steps to a successful strategy implementation process*. Available at https://www.cleverism.com/strategy-implementation-process/

Birnbaum, B. 2007. *Strategy implementation: Six supporting factors*. Available at www.birnbaumassociates.com/strategy-implementation.htm, 26.10.2007.

Bourgeois, L. J., & Brodwin, D. R. (1984). Strategic implementation: Five approaches to an elusive phenomenon. *Strategic Management Journal, 5*(3), 241–264. https://doi.org/10.1002/smj.4250050305.

Brenes, E. R., Mena, M., & Molina, G. E. (2008). Key success factors for strategy implementation in Latin America. *Journal of Business Research, 61*(6), 590–598.

Bryson, J. M., & Bromiley, P. (1993). Critical factors affecting the planning and implementation of major projects. *Strategic Management Journal, 14*(5), 319–337. https://doi.org/10.1002/smj.4250140502.

Cadwallader, S., Jarvis, C. B., Bitner, M. J., & Ostrom, A. L. (2010). Frontline employee motivation to participate in service innovation implementation. *Journal of the Academy of Marketing Science, 38*(2), 219–239. https://doi.org/10.1007/s11747-009-0151-3.

Cater, T., & Pucko, D. (2010). Factors of effective strategy implementation: Empirical evidence from Slovenian business practice. *Journal for East European Management Studies, 15*(3), 207–236.

Chartered Management Institute. (2014). *Implementing-strategy*. Available at https://www.managers.org.uk/wp-content/uploads/2020/03/CHK-259-Implementing-Strategy.pdf

Elbanna, S., & Fadol, Y. (2016). An analysis of the comprehensive implementation of strategic plans in emerging economies: The United Arab Emirates as a case study. *European Management Review, 13*(2), 75–89. https://doi.org/10.1111/emre.12068.

Farsight Leadership Organisation. (2007). *Strategy implementation and realisation*. Available at www.businessballs.com/businessstrategyimplementation.htm

Favaro, K. (2015). Defining strategy, implementation, and execution. *Harvard Business Review*. Available at https://hbr.org/2015/03/defining-strategy-implementation-and-execution

Fedato, G., Pires, V., & Trez, G. (2017). The future of research in strategy implementation in the BRICS context. *Brazilian Business Review, 14*(3), 288–303. https://doi.org/10.15728/bbr.2017.14.3.2.

Fulmer, W. E. (1990). Human resource management: The right hand of strategy implementation. *Human Resource Planning, 13*(1), 1–11.

Giles, W. D. (1991). Making strategy work. *Long Range Planning, 24*(5), 75–91.

Grundy, T. (1998). Strategy implementation and project management. *International Journal of Project Management, 16*(1), 43–50.

Hauc, A., & Kova, J. (2000). Project management in strategy implementation: Experiences in Slovenia. *International Journal of Project Management, 18*(1), 61–67.

Hrebiniak, L. G. (2005). *Making strategy work: Leading effective execution and change*. Upper Saddle River, NJ: Wharton School Publishing.

Hrebiniak, L. G. (2006). Obstacles to effective strategy implementation. *Organizational Dynamics, 35*(1), 12–31. https://doi.org/10.1016/j.orgdyn.2005.12.001.

Hrebiniak, L. G., & Joyce, W. F. (1984). *Implementing strategy*. New York: Macmillan Publishing.

Kaplan, R. S., & Norton, D. P. (1996). *The balanced scorecard: Translating strategy into action*. Boston: Harvard Business School Press.

Kaplan, R. S., & Norton, D. P. (2005). The office of strategy management. *Harvard Business Review, 83*(10), 72–80.

Kaplan, R. S., & Norton, D. P. (2006). How to implement a new strategy without disrupting your organization. *Harvard Business Review, 84*(3), 100–109.

Köseoglu, M. A., Altin, M., Chan, E., & Aladag, O. F. (2020). What are the key success factors for strategy formulation and implementation? Perspectives of managers in the hotel industry. *International Journal of Hospitality Management, 89*, 1–9. https://doi.org/10.1016/j.ijhm.2020.102574.

Kova, J. (1996). Poveanje uinkovitosti uresnievanja strategije podjetja s pomojo projektnega managementa. *The Organ, 29*(2), 94–99.

Lahkar, R., & Mukherjee, S. (2020). Dominant strategy implementation in a large population public goods game. *Economics Letters, 197*, 109616. https://doi.org/10.1016/j.econlet.2020.109616.

Lemarleni, J. E., Ochieng, I., Gakobo, T., & Mwaura, P. (2017). Effects of resource allocation on strategy implementation at Kenya Police Service in Nairobi County. *International Academic Journal of Human Resource and Business Administration, 2*(4), 1–26. http://www.iajournals.org/articles/iajhrba_v2_i4_1_26.pdf.

Lindsay, S., Jack, G., & Ambrosini, V. (2018). A critical diversity framework to better educate students about strategy implementation. *Academy of Management Learning and Education, 17* (3), 241–258. https://doi.org/10.5465/amle.2017.0150.

Lorange, P. (1982). *Implementation of strategic planning*. Englewood Cliffs: Prentice Hall.

Mailu, R. N., Ntale, J. F., & Ngui, T. K. (2018). Strategy implementation and organizational performance in the pharmaceutical industry in Kenya. *International Academic Journal of Human Resource and Business Administration, 3*(2), 33–47. http://www.iajournals.org/articles/iajhrba_v3_i2_33_47.pdf.

Miller, K. (2020). A managers guide to successful strategy implementation. *Business Insight Blogs*. Available at https://online.hbs.edu/blog/post/strategy-implementation-for-managers

Minarro-Viseras, E., Baines, T., & Sweeney, M. (2005). Key success factors when implementing strategic manufacturing initiatives. *International Journal of Operations and Production Management, 25*(2), 151–179.

Nicholls, J. (1994). The strategic leadership star: A guiding light in delivering value to the customer. *Management Decision, 32*(8), 21–26.

Noble, C. H. (1999a). The eclectic roots of strategy implementation research. *Journal of Business Research, 45*(2), 119–134.

Noble, C. H. (1999b). Building the strategy implementation network. *Business Horizons, 42*(6), 19–19. https://go.gale.com/ps/i.do?p=AONE&sw=w&issn=00076813&v=2.1&it=r&id=GALE%7CA58381515&sid=googleScholar&linkaccess=fulltext.

Nwachukwu, C., Chladkova, H., & Fadeyi, O. (2018). Strategy formulation process and innovation performance nexus. *International Journal for Quality Research, 12*(1), 147–164. https://doi.org/10.18421/IJQR12.01-09.

Obeidat, B. Y., Al-Hadidi, A., Tarhini, A., & Masa'deh, R. (2017). Factors affecting strategy implementation: A case study of pharmaceutical companies in the middle east. *Review of*

International Business and Strategy, 27(3), 386–408. https://doi.org/10.1108/RIBS-10-2016-0065.
Okumus, F. (2001). Towards a strategy implementation framework. *International Journal of Contemporary Hospitality Management, 13*(7), 327–338. https://doi.org/10.1108/09596110110403712.
Olson, E. M., Slater, S. F., & Hult, G. T. M. (2005). The importance of structure and process to strategy implementation. *Business Horizons, 48*(1), 47–54. https://doi.org/10.1016/j.bushor.2004.10.002.
Olson, E. M., Slater, S. F., Hult, G. T. M., & Olson, K. M. (2018). The application of human resource management policies within the marketing organization: The impact on business and marketing strategy implementation. *Industrial Marketing Management, 69*, 62–73. https://doi.org/10.1016/j.indmarman.2018.01.029.
Pellegrinelli, S., & Bowman, C. (1994). Implementing strategy through projects. *Long Range Planning, 27*(4), 125–132.
Piórkowska, N. and Ryńca, R. 2020. *Factors affecting the process of strategy implementation in public and non-public schools in Wroclaw.* https://doi.org/10.29119/1641-3466.2020.149.41
Pitt, C. S., & Treen, E. (2017). Understanding communication in disaster response: A marketing strategy formulation and implementation perspective. *Journal of Public Affairs, 17*(3), e1639. https://doi.org/10.1002/pa.1639.
Puko, D. (2006). *Strateško upravljanje*. Ljubljana: Ekonomska fakulteta.
Satyro, W. C., Sacomano, J. B., Contador, J. C., Almeida, C. M. V. B., & Giannetti, B. F. (2017). Process of strategy formulation for sustainable environmental development: Basic model. *Journal of Cleaner Production, 166*, 1295–1304. https://doi.org/10.1016/j.jclepro.2017.08.128.
Simons, R. 2010. Seven strategy questions: A simple approach for better execution. *Harvard Business Review*. Available at https://hbswk.hbs.edu/item/seven-strategy-questions-a-simple-approach-for-better-execution
Speculand, R. (2006). The great big strategy challenge. *Strategic Direction, 22*(3), 3–5.
Tawse, A., & Tabesh, P. (2021). Strategy implementation: A review and an introductory framework. *European Management Journal, 39*(1), 22–33. https://doi.org/10.1016/j.emj.2020.09.005.
Ulrich, D. (1998). A new mandate for human resources. *Harvard Business Review, 76*(1), 124–134.
Wheelen, T. L., & Hunger, D. J. (2006). *Concepts in strategic management and business policy*. Upper Saddle River: Pearson – Prentice Hall.

Machine Learning in Strategy and Implementation

5

5.1 Introduction

Chapter 4 discussed strategy implementation. From the onset, it highlighted some key definitions of strategy implementation. Following the definitions, a brief distinction between strategy implementation and strategy execution was considered. Some activities in strategy implementation were briefly outlined, and some factors that firms need to consider as they implement strategies were discussed. The last part of the chapter outlined the typical pitfalls and mitigations for successful strategy implementation.

In recent times, ML has become one of the most influential and robust technologies. According to Edwards (2018), ML is used to turn information into knowledge in modern times. The rise of ML is supported by the explosion of data in the past 50 years. In the past, this data was not analysed, understood or used effectively to find patterns hidden within it.

The rise of ML techniques has meant that it can be used to find valuable underlying patterns within complex data automatically. Alpaydin (2020) notes that humans could otherwise struggle to discover these hidden patterns. The output and knowledge generated from this can predict future events and perform all kinds of complex decision-making (Alpaydin, 2020).

ML is different from other traditional software. Traditional software would typically combine human-created rules with data to create answers to a problem. ML uses data and answers to discover the rules behind a problem (Chollet, 2017). This chapter explores the role of ML in strategy formulation and strategy implementation.

The chapter provides an overview of the concept of ML in Sect. 5.2. This is followed by a discussion of the growing influence of ML in Sect. 5.3. Section 5.4 outlines the forms of ML. A brief overview of deep learning is introduced in Sect. 5.5, while Sect. 5.6 explores ML in strategy and strategy implementation.

T. Moloi, T. Marwala, *Artificial Intelligence and the Changing Nature of Corporations*, Future of Business and Finance,
https://doi.org/10.1007/978-3-030-76313-8_5

5.2 Understanding Machine Learning

According to Jordan and Mitchell (2015), ML is a concept that addresses the question related to how to construct computers that are capable of improving automatically through experience. ML is therefore a discipline that focusses on two interrelated questions, namely:

- What fundamental statistical-computational-information-theoretic principles govern all learning systems such as computers, firms and humans?
- How can one construct computer systems capable of automatically improving via experience? (Jordan & Mitchell, 2015)

According to Edwards (2018), ML is the concept of an algorithm at the centre of computer programming. An algorithm refers to a sequence of instructions that should be carried out to convert the input to an output. Alpaydin (2020) notes that several algorithms for many tasks have been devised. However, algorithms for some tasks are yet to be devised despite decades of research. Some of the tasks that do not have algorithms can be effortlessly accomplished by humans without being aware of how they do them.

Marshall (2019) views ML as computer programs that enable computer networks to discover patterns hidden in vast amounts of data such as text, audio and video. Data emanating from the text, audio and video (and other sources) is sometimes referred to as big data. According to Barpaga (2019), ML can be understood to be the science and branch of AI where computers are trained from data to perform a particular task rather than by explicitly programming them. The process in ML involves humans training the machines from past data to do what humans can do.

Edwards (2018) indicates that computers are programmed to optimise a performance criterion for ML to occur using example data or past experience. Accordingly, there should be a model defined up to some parameters. Learning is the execution of a computer program to optimise the parameters of the model using the training data or past experience (Alpaydin, 2020). The model itself may either be predictive or descriptive. If it is predictive, it makes predictions, and if it is descriptive, it gains knowledge from data.

ML methods can be applied to an extensive database. This process is called data mining. According to Edwards (2018), the application of the analogy is that a large volume of earth and raw materials is extracted from a mine which, when processed, lead to a small amount of very precious material. As such, in data mining, a large volume of data would be processed to construct a simple model with practical use, such as having high predictive accuracy.

For Priyadharshini (2020), without direct programming, ML applications, like humans, learn from experience. When ML applications are exposed to new data, these applications learn, grow, change and develop by themselves. Accordingly, with ML, computers find insightful information without being told where to look. They find insightful information by leveraging algorithms that learn from data in an iterative process. Priyadharshini (2020) indicates that ML applications learn from previous computations and transactions and use pattern recognition to produce reliable and informed results.

5.3 The Growing Influence of Machine Learning

Jordan and Mitchell (2015) have attributed the growth and progress in ML to online data availability and low-cost computation. Examples of low-cost computation include the Hadoop platform, which, essentially, this platform provides distributed cloud data hosting and processing capabilities. Adopting data-intensive machine learning techniques can be traced through science, technology and commerce, leading to more evidence-based decision-making through many works of day-to-day life. Examples of these include health care, manufacturing, marketing, policing, financial modelling and education.

According to Jordan and Mitchell (2015), the field of machine learning has progressed significantly over the last couple of decades. In the past, it was just individuals being curious in a laboratory. Now, it is more practical technology, and this technology is used widely in the commercial space. ML is the method of choice in AI because of data availability (Moloi & Marwala, 2020). Jordan and Mitchell (2015) indicate that ML has been used to develop helpful software for natural language processing, robot control, speech recognition, computer vision and other applications.

5.4 Forms of Machine Learning

There are three forms of ML, namely, supervised learning, unsupervised learning and reinforcement learning. The three use different approaches, but they all follow the same underlying process and theory. The process includes data collection, data preparation, training, evaluation and tuning as explained below:

- The first step in the process includes the collection of data that the algorithm uses to learn.
- The second involves formatting and engineering data into the optimal format. During this process, the essential features of data are extracted, and dimensional reduction is performed.
- The third step is training, also known as the fitting stage. The ML algorithm learns through the data that has been collected and prepared.
- The fourth involves testing the model to see how well it performs.
- The last step involves fine-tuning the model to maximise its performance.

5.4.1 A Brief Overview of Supervised Learning

According to Priyadharshini (2020), supervised learning uses known or labelled data as training data. Since the data is known, the learning is supervised and directed towards a known outcome for successful execution. Typically, the input data will be loaded through the ML algorithm to train the model. Once the model is successfully trained based on the known data, unknown data can be inputted into the model to get a new response. Figure 5.1 illustrates a typical supervised learning process.

Alpaydin (2020) uses the example of the weather forecast and beach visiting by bathers to understand the supervised ML process. Accordingly, the weather would be an input, and bathers to the beach are an output. In this case, ML is trying to learn the relationship between the weather and beach visitors. Clearly, in this example, data is labelled to teach the model how to figure out patterns, hence the supervised learning for the ML algorithms.

In this example, Alpaydin (2020) indicates that the new inputs of forecast temperature can then be fed into the ML algorithm. This generates an output of a future prediction of the number of visitors. Therefore, the ability of ML to adapt to new inputs and make predictions is the crucial generalisation part of ML.

The generated output could be categorised as a finite set, for instance, low, medium and high. In Alpaydin's (2020) example, the typical supervised learning process would be represented by Fig. 5.2.

Figure 5.2 illustrates the case where ML is deciding how to classify the input. Alpaydin (2020) describes this as classification. According to Glose (2018),

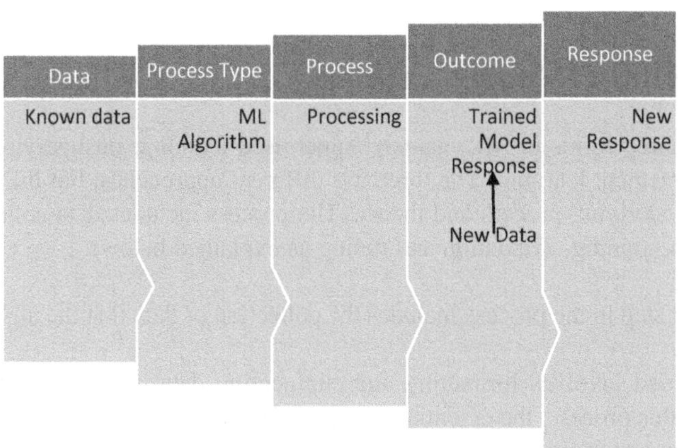

Fig. 5.1 Typical supervised learning process. Source: Authors own illustration, adapted from Priyadharshini (2020)

Temperature→ML Algorithm →Processing →Trained Model →visitors

Fig. 5.2 Typical supervised learning process. Source: Authors own illustration, adapted from Alpaydin (2020)

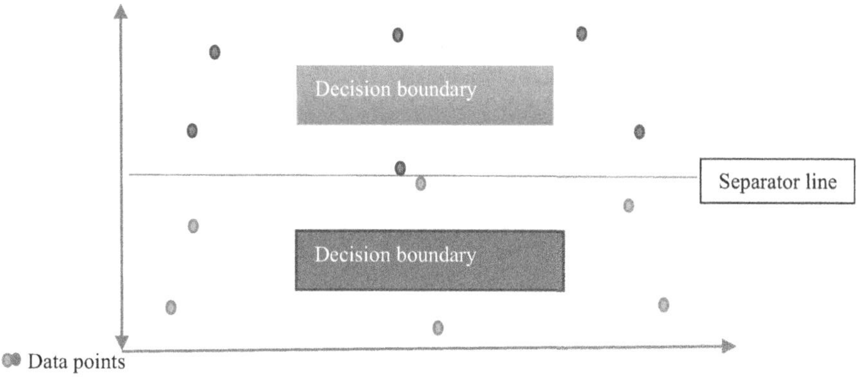

Fig. 5.3 Separator lines, decision boundaries and decision surface. Source: Authors' own illustration; Adapted from Glose (2018)

30^{0c}→ML Algorithm →Processing →Trained Model →10 000

Fig. 5.4 Typical supervised learning process. Source: Authors own illustration, adapted from Alpaydin (2020)

classification is used to group similar data points into different sections to classify them. ML is used to find the rules that explain how to separate the different data points. There are multiple ways to discover these rules.

These multiple ways focus on using data and answers to discover rules that linearly separate data points. Classification approaches attempt to find the best way to separate data points with a separator line. The separator lines drawn between classes are known as the decision boundaries. The area that is chosen to define a class is known as the decision surface. If a data point falls within the boundaries of the decision surface, it will be assigned a particular class. We illustrate the classification approaches in Fig. 5.3

Earlier, we discussed generated output and indicated that it could be categorised as a finite set, for instance low, medium and high. The alternative output could also be a number. Alpaydin (2020) refers to this as regression. Regression is useful when predicting number-based problems, such as the probability of an event occurring and stock market movements. In finance, regression is commonly used to find the patterns in stocks and other assets so that investors could decide when to hold, buy or sell.

Keshari (2020) emphasises that both the classification and regression supervised learning techniques can be extended to much more complex tasks, such as those involving speech and audio, image classification, object detection and Chatbots. In Alpaydin's (2020) example of weather, the typical supervised learning process would be represented by Fig. 5.4.

Alpaydin (2020) warns that there is a risk of overtraining the model. The risk is that there could be overfitting to the examples used, and the model would fail to adapt to new and previously unseen inputs. Another challenge with supervised learning is that it usually requires many data points before it learns. Thus, obtaining sufficient reliably labelled data is often the most challenging and most expensive part of using this form of learning.

5.4.2 A Brief Overview of Unsupervised Learning

According to Priyadharshini (2020), unsupervised learning will be characterised by the unknown and unlabelled training data. Based on this, the input cannot be guided to the algorithm. To train the model, unlabelled data would be fed into the ML algorithm. The model uses the unlabelled data to search for a pattern and give the desired response.

Edwards (2018) concurs that only input data is provided in the examples and there are no labelled example outputs to aim for in the unsupervised learning process. Typically, Edwards (2018) believes that unsupervised learning will mostly be useful when conducting exploratory data analysis.

Typically, density estimation is used to find exciting structures in unlabelled data. Accordingly, the most common form of density estimation is clustering. Priyadharshini (2020) indicates that clustering is the act of creating groups with differing characteristics and an attempt to find various subgroups within a dataset. According to Glose (2018), there ordinarily will be no restriction on the number of sets of data and clusters to create since this is unsupervised learning.

Figure 5.5 illustrates the typical unsupervised learning process.

Unknown data→ ML Algorithm →Processing →Trained Model →Response

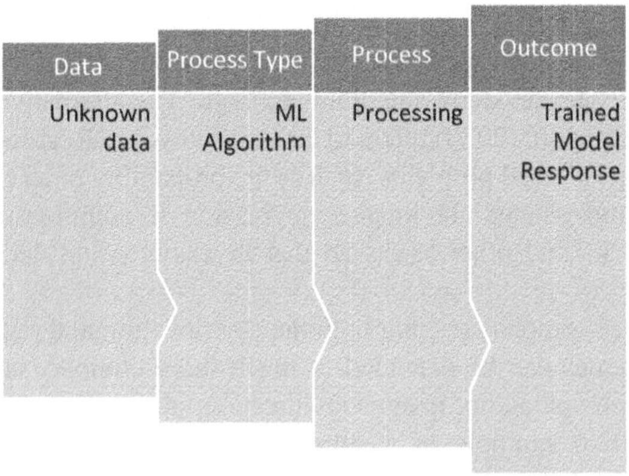

Fig. 5.5 Typical unsupervised learning process. Source: Authors own illustration, adapted from Priyadharshini (2020)

5.4.3 A Brief Overview of Reinforcement Learning

According to Edwards (2018), a typical reinforcement learning process occurs where the algorithm discovers data through a process of trial and error. The reinforcement learning process does not use labels but instead uses rewards to learn. Reinforcement learning occurs when the agent chooses actions that maximise the expected reward over a given time (Priyadharshini, 2020).

Therefore, the reward-motivated behaviour is key in reinforcement learning. Edwards (2018) indicates that there are three major components that make up the reinforcement learning:

- The agent—this will be a learner or decision-maker in the ecosystem.
- The environment—the environment includes everything that the agent interacts with.
- The actions—this refers to the performance of the agent.

Figure 5.6 illustrates the major role players in the reinforcement learning process.

To illustrate this, Glose (2018) uses an example of a robot placed in an environment with roads and obstacles. The goal of this robot will be to move from point A to point B. Every step it takes results in either earning a reward point (+1) or a penalty on hitting an obstacle (−1). Accordingly, with every iteration, the robot will learn from mistakes by hitting possible obstacles and figures out the optimal path. A typical reward-penalty system is illustrated in Fig. 5.7.

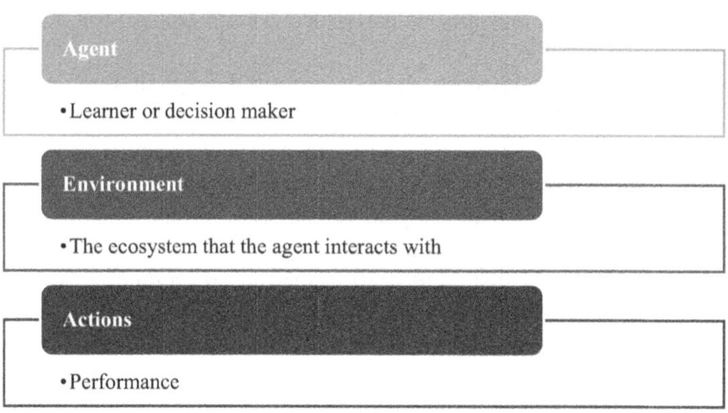

Fig. 5.6 Major role players in the reinforcement learning process. Source: Authors own illustration

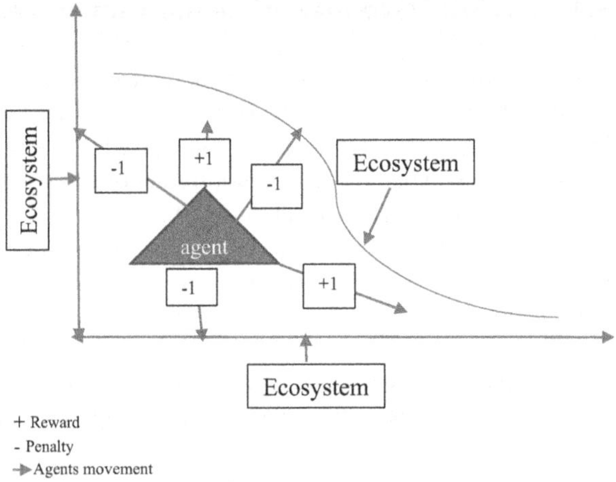

Fig. 5.7 Typical reward-penalty system. Source: Authors' own illustration

5.5 A Brief Overview of Deep Learning

According to Sejnowski (2020), deep learning was inspired by the massively parallel architecture found in the brains. Accordingly, the DL origins can be traced to Frank Rosenblatt's book, *Perceptrons and the Theory of Brain Mechanics* (Rosenblatt, 1961), published in the early 1960s. Sejnowski (2020) states that initially, DL was based on a simplified model of a single neuron proposed by McCulloch and Pitts' (1943) treatise *A logical calculus of the ideas immanent in nervous activity*. Therefore, Rosenblatt's (1961) perceptrons performed pattern recognition and learned to classify labelled examples.

There are two types of learning, deep learning (DL) and shallow learning (SL). Accordingly, SL would typically contain the single-layer neural networks, whereas DL would contain many layers of neural networks. According to Freiherr (2019), the DL network would typically contain lots of computational nodes as well as lots of layers of those nodes, whereas a shallower network means that there are fewer computations so it is less math going on.

Lloyd (2015) points out that the depth is what requires a number of node layers. With this, there is need for more computation power for forward or backward optimisation while training, testing and eventually running these neural networks (Genc, 2019).

In addition to the need for more computation power for forward or backward optimisation while training, testing and eventually running these neural networks, Piekniewski (2019) warns that deep networks are black boxes which most people have no idea how to work.

According to Chauhan et al. (2019), DL methods are slowly gaining popularity. The reasons for this popularity are because they often outperform shallow ML methods which often consist of single neural networks. Using their power, they

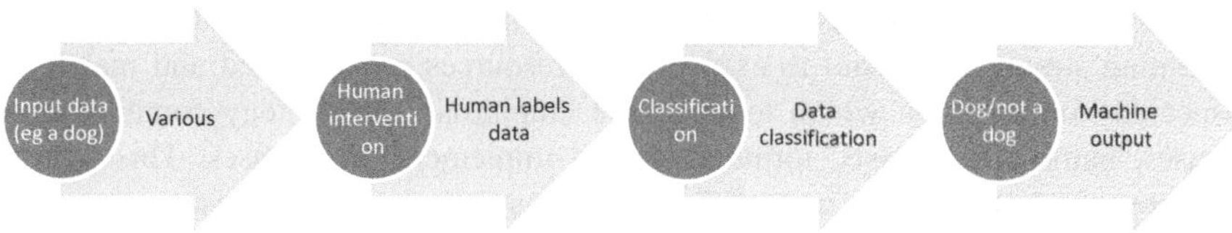

Fig. 5.8 A typical shallow learning process (human intervention). Source: Authors Own Illustration, adapted from Jagreet (2018)

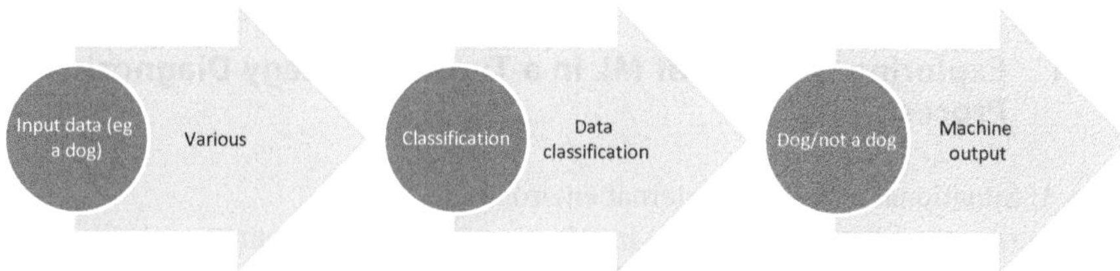

Fig. 5.9 A typical deep learning process (no human intervention). Source: Authors Own Illustration, adapted from Jagreet (2018)

are able to automatically extract features from raw data with little or no need for pre-processing.

Sejnowski (2020) suggests that the popularity of DL methods is going to sour given the information age with loads of data gushing from sensors and the available sources for pipelines turning this data into information, and information into knowledge, and then knowledge into understanding and, ultimately, knowledge into wisdom. Figures 5.8 and 5.9 illustrate the difference between deep and shallow learning.

5.6 Machine Learning in Strategy and Strategy Implementation

The concept of strategy was discussed in Chap. 3. From the business perspective, it was indicated that strategy refers to a way in which firms explain to their stakeholders how they will be moving forward. Accordingly, it was indicated that the firm strategy is generally viewed as a course of action that can help the firm in attaining their objectives. There are three aspects of strategy formulation, namely:

- Corporate-level strategy
- The competitive strategy (sometimes called the business strategy)
- The parenting strategy

Accordingly, it was emphasised that the growth or directional strategy outlines the growth objective of the firm and mainly on how to achieve this. On its part, a point was made that the portfolio strategy outlines the portfolio of the lines of the firm, which assist in the diversification in which the business should engage. The parenting strategy was said to explain how resources are allocated and managed, especially on areas on which to put more emphasis. The strategy contains three phases, namely, diagnosis, formulation and implementation phases. This section explores the role of ML in traditional business processes such as strategy and strategy implementation. It explores the role of ML in the diagnosis, formulation and implementation phases.

5.6.1 Exploring the Role of ML in a Typical Strategy Diagnosis Process

Step A: Situational analysis of internal environment

Description of Step A: Diagnosis involves carrying out a situation analysis where the firm's internal environment is analysed, including identifying and evaluating the current mission, strategic objectives, strategies and results, including significant strengths and weaknesses.

Role of ML in Step A: The situation analysis would require that a firm process the stored internal data to extract value from it. The massive volume of data required to evaluate and inform the mission, strategic objectives, strategies and strengths and weaknesses of a firm would typically be complex if it were to be done manually and by a human being. ML can take supervised learning, unsupervised learning and reinforcement learning form as explained during the discussions. The process includes data collection, data preparation, training, evaluation and tuning in all these types of learning. It is clear here that as algorithms receive data, they will learn and understand the firm better. What is further clear is that the stored internal data comes in both structured and unstructured way. These massive amounts of data are troublesome for traditional methods. The abilities of ML to handle this type of data are important for a firm to uncover key trends and patterns within data to provide further insights that are crucial in crafting the mission, strategic objectives, strategies, desired results and significant strengths and weaknesses. Table 5.1

Table 5.1 Difference between two firms, one deploying ML for big data analysis and the other does not

	Firm A	Firm B	Consequence	Competitive advantage
Application of ML in big data analysis	×	✓	The firm applying ML in Big Data Analytics is able to uncover key trends and patterns within data	The firm applying ML in Big Data Analytics gains insights that are crucial in crafting the mission, strategic objectives, strategies, desired results and significant strengths and weaknesses facing the firm

Source: Authors' own illustration

Table 5.2 Difference between two firms, one deploying ML for big data analysis and the other not

	Firm A	Firm B	Consequence	ML advantage
Application of ML in big data analysis	×	✓	The firm applying ML in Big Data Analytics is able to uncover key trends and patterns within external data	The firm applying ML in Big Data Analytics gains insights that are crucial in crafting the mission, strategic objectives, strategies, desired results and significant opportunities and threats facing the firm

Source: Authors' own illustration

illustrates a typical example of the external situational analysis of two firms, one deploying ML for big data analysis and the other not.

Step B: Situational analysis of external environment

Description of Step B: The strategy diagnosis further involves the analysis of the firm's external environment, which comprises opportunities and threats. It also involves the analysis of the firm's external environment, which also includes the major opportunities and threats. Lastly, diagnosis involves the identification of the critical issues, which are sometimes two to five of the major problems, threats, weaknesses and opportunities that demand high priority and attention.

Role of ML in Step B: The situation analysis would require that a firm process the available external data to extract value from it. This data could come from industry sources, national and international statistical agencies, business news, securities exchange news services, expert opinions, etc. The massive volume of data required to evaluate and inform the mission, strategic objectives, strategies and major opportunities and threats of a firm would typically be complex if they were to be done manually and by a human being. As explained earlier, ML can take supervised learning, unsupervised learning and reinforcement learning form. The typical process includes data collection, data preparation, training, evaluation and tuning in all these types of learning. These massive amounts of data are troublesome and very time-consuming, if traditional methods are deployed. The ability of ML to handle this type of data is important for a firm to uncover key trends and patterns within data to provide further insights that are crucial for crafting the mission, strategic objectives, strategies, desired results and significant opportunities and threats. Table 5.2 illustrates a typical example of the external situational analysis of two firms, one deploying ML for big data analysis and the other not.

5.6.2 Exploring the Role of ML in a Typical Strategy Formulation Process

Step A: Objective setting

Description of Step A: Analysis of each factor that influences the selection of objectives.

Table 5.3 Difference between two firms, one deploying ML for big data analysis and the other not

	Firm A	Firm B	Consequence	ML advantage
Application of ML in big data analysis	×	✓	There are potentially various factors influencing the selection of objectives by each firm. This could be time-consuming if done manually as each of them has to be assessed, analysed and considered for a decision to be taken. ML is wired to deal with the formulation of potential scenarios, which could then be analysed for the best option to be chosen	The firm applying ML in Big Data Analytics gains an advantage as objectives emanating from a data-intensive and data-informed process are risk calibrated. Furthermore, several factors influencing the selection of objectives would have been considered

Source: Authors' own illustration

Role of ML in Step A: The analysis of each factor that influences the selection of objectives will be a cumbersome process for traditional methods that have previously relied on human beings. There could potentially be numerous factors influencing the selection of objectives. Each of them has to be assessed, analysed and considered for a decision to be taken. These are many datasets, which ML is wired to deal with for the formulation of potential scenarios which could then be analysed and the best option be chosen. Objectives emanating from the process that is data-intensive and data-informed are risk calibrated, as several factors that influence the selection of objectives would have been considered. In Table 5.3, we illustrate a typical example of objective setting of two firms, one deploying ML for big data analysis and the other not.

Step B: Internal and external context

Description of Step B: Analysis of general economic and industrial environment in which the firm operates. It involves analysis of the competition and its movement. Furthermore, it involves analysis of the strengths, weaknesses, threats and opportunities.

Role of ML in Step B: As noted earlier, ML is wired to deal with big data, which would otherwise be a cumbersome process for a human being or for traditional methods. The analysis of general economic and industrial environments in which the firm operates, the competition, and its movement as well as the firm's strengths, weaknesses, threats and opportunities require massive data handling, labelling and integration to formulate potential scenarios. The ability of ML to handle massive data is important for a firm to uncover key trends and patterns within data, which is important for insights into data. These insights are crucial in assisting a firm in formulating potential scenarios. In Table 5.4, we illustrate a typical example of the consideration of external and internal environments by two firms, one deploying ML for big data analysis and the other not.

Step C: Target setting

Table 5.4 Difference between two firms, one deploying ML for big data analysis and the other not

	Firm A	Firm B	Consequence	ML advantage
Application of ML in big data analysis	×	✓	Since the analysis of general economic and industrial environments in which the firm operates, the competition and its movement is a cumbersome process, ML provides a powerful tool for the analysis of structured and unstructured data in order for the firm to gauge its strengths, weaknesses, threats and opportunities properly. This requires massive data handling, labelling and integration; ML is capable of doing this and the formulation of potential scenarios	The firm applying ML in Big Data Analytics gains an advantage in the analysis of internal and external environments. Strengths, weaknesses, threats and opportunities that emanate from a process that is data-intensive and data-informed are risk calibrated. Furthermore, several factors that influence the selection of objectives are based on the properly formulated scenarios

Source: Authors' own illustration

Description of Step C: Setting the target against each stated objective

Role of ML in Step C: Setting targets requires that the firm understand its key stakeholder needs. Each of objective is translated into goals, which subsequently addresses the firm's key stakeholder needs. The firm's operations would rely on each other to ensure that the bigger goal is achieved. The finance department relies on the sales department to drive the sales, and the sales department will in turn rely on the finance department to ensure that marketing and advertising invoices are paid on time and that the finance provides it with management accounts to see how far it is from its targets. This example would typically represent the firm's internal interdependencies. External stakeholders such as customers also need to be understood in terms of what product they are leaning towards and what informs such a leaning. There is also a need to understand what this incline means for a firm. The ML user modelling platforms could be used to mine data of this nature, which could subsequently allow a firm to make an informed decision. In Table 5.5, we illustrate a typical example of target setting by two firms, one deploying ML for big data analysis and the other not.

Step D: Segmentation of plans

Description of Step D: Objectives are cascaded to each segment of the firm/ business, based on the contribution that each segment makes to the strategic objective.

Role of ML in Step D: Similar to the target setting, the segmentation of plans requires an understanding of what each segment is capable of (segment capabilities). It further requires an understanding of the segment dependencies. To formulate this understanding, a firm requires many structured and unstructured datasets, which ML

Table 5.5 Difference between two firms, one deploying ML for big data analysis and the other not

	Firm A	Firm B	Consequence	ML advantage
Application of ML in big data analysis	×	✓	A firm will have a better idea of needs of the key stakeholders. It will also have better calibrated data for understanding both internal and external stakeholders. These are all crucial aspects in target setting	The firm applying ML, specifically a tool such as the ML user modelling platforms, could mine key stakeholder data, which could subsequently allow a firm to make an intelligent and informed decision

Source: Authors' own illustration

Table 5.6 Difference between two firms, one deploying ML for big data analysis and the other not

	Firm A	Firm B	Consequence	ML advantage
Application of ML in big data analysis	×	✓	A firm will have a better idea of its internal dependencies and capabilities. It will also have better calibrated data for understanding external stakeholders. These are all crucial aspects in target setting	The firm applying ML, specifically a tool such as the ML user modelling platforms, could mine key stakeholder data, which could subsequently allow a firm to make an intelligent and informed decision

Source: Authors' own illustration

is wired to deal with for the understanding of capabilities and dependencies. The segmentation of plans emanating from the process that is data-intensive and data-informed is risk calibrated based on capabilities and dependencies of the firm's segments. In Table 5.6, we illustrate a typical example of segmentation by two firms, one deploying ML for big data analysis and the other not.

Step E: Performance review

Description of Step E: Performance is reviewed in order to understand the gap between the actual performance and the planned or desired performance. This requires analysis of past performances and projections for the future.

Role of ML in Step E: This step requires that data be analysed to pick up the gaps between the desired and the actual goals. Big data will provide insights relating to the factors that have contributed to the achievement or non-achievement of the desired performance. The decision can then be made as to where resources need to be ploughed to improve performance or to leverage the process so that it yields even better results. Automated systems are also able to report the performance in real time. Should the senior leadership team wish to see performance at a certain period, they need not wait for reporting timelines. In Table 5.7, we illustrate a typical example of analysing performance by two firms, one deploying ML for big data analysis and the other not.

Step F: Strategic choice

Table 5.7 Difference between two firms, one deploying ML for big data analysis and the other not

	Firm A	Firm B	Consequence	ML advantage
Application of ML in big data analysis	×	✓	Big data will provide insights relating to the factors that have contributed to the achievement or non-achievement of the desired performance. These factors could then be analysed to make informed decisions	The firm applying ML in Big Data Analytics gains an advantage in the analysis of internal and external environments to understand the factors that drive performance. Decisions to whether to supplement the process are data-intensive and data-informed. They are risk calibrated. Furthermore, factors influencing the selection of performance are vast, containing both internal and external data, structured and unstructured data

Source: Authors' own illustration

Table 5.8 Difference between two firms, one deploying ML for big data analysis and the other not

	Firm A	Firm B	Consequence	ML advantage
Application of ML in big data analysis	×	✓	Big data will provide insights relating to the key factors driving the strategic choice for the achievement of the desired performance	The firm applying ML in Big Data Analytics gains an advantage in the in-depth analysis of major key factors that drive the choice of strategy to be followed. Decisions on the strategic choice are data-intensive and data-informed. The risks of the choice have been carefully calibrated

Source: Authors' own illustration

Description of Step F: Following the analysis of various options, the firm will make a strategic choice after having understood its strengths, weaknesses, threats and opportunities.

Role of ML in Step F: The strategic choice will be a function of understanding vast sets of data, which are converted to information by ML algorithms. These include the internal and external contexts; macroeconomic factors; the industry in which the company operates; the strengths, weaknesses, opportunities, threats, interdependencies and key internal and external stakeholders; behaviour of competitors; behaviour of clients; targets; and performance measures among other key things. In Table 5.8, we illustrate a typical example of constructing a strategic choice by two firms, one deploying ML for big data analysis and the other not.

5.6.3 Exploring the Role of ML in a Typical Strategy Implementation Process

Step A: Ensuring that plans are well aligned to the firm's mission, vision and values

Description of Step A: This step ensures that the implementation of plans is premised on the objectives and strategy of the firm.

Role of ML in Step A: This step is similar to the process of performance analysis; the difference is that the analyses are being done on the alignment side of things. Data are analysed to pick up the gaps between the mission, values and vision. This data could come from various sources that speak to the firm's value system, mission and vision. This data will be both structured and unstructured. Mapping this data to ensure that there is alignment to these three crucial aspects of strategy could be time-consuming if traditional methods are deployed. The ability of ML to handle this type of data is important for a firm to uncover key trends and patterns within data to provide further insights that are crucial in aligning the mission, vision and values. In Table 5.9, we illustrate a typical example of aligning the mission, vision and the values by a pair of firms, one deploying ML for big data analysis and the other not.

Step B: Building an effective leadership team

Description of Step B: This step is critical because optimal implementation of a strategy is premised on professionals, especially their management and leadership capacity of strategic and operational managers. In this step, it is also important for leaders to adjust their leadership styles as well as learn management techniques and approaches. Adjustment of leadership style is important because strategy implementation can alter priorities, change resource allocation and even shift relationships,

Table 5.9 Difference between two firms, one deploying ML for big data analysis and the other not

	Firm A	Firm B	Consequence	ML advantage
Application of ML in big data analysis	×	✓	Data are analysed to pick up gaps between the mission, values and the vision. Various sources speak to the firm's value system, mission and vision. Therefore, data will be both structured and unstructured. Mapping this data to ensure that there is alignment to these three crucial aspects of strategy could be time-consuming if traditional methods are deployed	The disadvantage of a firm not applying ML in Big Data Analytics is the potential misalignment between the firm's vision, mission and values. The misalignment could lead to the failure to track progress towards the achievement of the firm's goals. The firm deploying ML gains an advantage associated with uncovering key trends and patterns within data to provide further insights that are crucial in aligning the mission, vision and values

Source: Authors' own illustration

Table 5.10 Difference between two firms, one deploying ML for big data analysis and the other not

	Firm A	Firm B	Consequence	ML advantage
Application of ML in big data analysis	×	✓	Big data will provide insights relating to the factors contributing to the achievement or non-achievement of the desired performance. These factors could then be analysed to change the stance of the firm's leadership	The firm applying ML in Big Data Analytics gains an advantage in the analysis of internal and external environments to understand the factors driving performance. Decisions on whether to supplement the process are data-intensive and data-informed. Leadership changes its stance as informed by data. The changes in stance are risk calibrated. Furthermore, factors influencing the decision to change are vast, containing both internal and external data, structured and unstructured data

Source: Authors' own illustration

which can bring threats to the power and status of some influential people within the firm.

Role of ML in Step B: We see the role of ML as the provision of key insights relating to the factors contributing to the achievement of the desired performance. The performance information coming through from operations indicates where resources need to be ploughed to improve performance or to leverage the process so that it yields even better results. This requires that the firm has access to the information on an ongoing basis and that the firm has a nimble style of leadership. The nimble leadership style is the one that allows adjustment of certain positions, should data point to the need for adjustment. Automated systems are also crucial in reporting performance in real time. Should senior leadership wish to see performance at a certain period, they need not wait for reporting timelines. In Table 5.10, we illustrate a typical example of effective leadership informed by data of two firms, one deploying ML for big data analysis and the other not.

Step C: Formulating the implementation plan

Description of Step C: This step requires that the full implementation plan is created for the firm and, more importantly, for all the levels of the firm. The implementation plan should state the resources required and the steps needed to attain the objectives. The financial resources, personnel and operational and technological resources required should be quantified, and the plan should identify the people responsible for individual initiatives. The implementation plan assists in setting priorities, accountabilities and the short-term and long-term objectives of

Table 5.11 Difference between two firms, one deploying ML for big data analysis and the other does not

	Firm A	Firm B	Consequence	ML advantage
Application of ML in big data analysis	×	✓	Data is analysed and quantified to understand the financial resources, personnel and operational and technological resources required. Mapping this data ensures that there is life in the implementation plan, which could otherwise be time-consuming if traditional methods are deployed	The disadvantage of a firm not applying ML in Big Data Analytics is the potential misalignment between the different key resources required to deliver the strategy. The misalignment could lead to the failure to track progress towards the achievement of the firm's goals. The firm deploying ML gains an advantage associated with uncovering key trends and patterns within data to provide further insights that are crucial in aligning and identifying key priorities, accountabilities and the short-term and long-term objectives of the firm

Source: Authors' own illustration

the firm. Personal accountabilities are critical in the implementation plan so that individuals understand their responsibilities. The implementation plan should also be visible so that it does not become disconnected from the decision-making process and it should be accessible to everyone.

Role of ML in Step C: This step is similar to the process of performance alignment. Creating the overarching implementation plan is important for the identification of resources required and the steps that need to be followed to achieve the goals. Data is analysed to understand the financial resources, personnel and operational and technological resources required. This data is also quantified. The data could come from various sources, and they have to speak to the priorities, accountabilities and the short-term and long-term objectives of the firm. These data will be in structured and unstructured formats. Mapping these data ensures that there is life in the implementation plan, which could otherwise be time-consuming if traditional methods are deployed. The ability of ML to handle this type of data is important for a firm to uncover key trends and patterns within data to provide further insights that are crucial in identifying key priorities, accountabilities and the short-term and long-term objectives of the firm. In Table 5.11, we illustrate a typical example of aligning and identifying key priorities, accountabilities and the short-term as well as the long-term objectives of the firm. We use data from two firms, one deploying ML for big data analysis and the other not.

Step D: Allocation of budgetary resources

Table 5.12 Difference between two firms, one deploying ML for big data analysis and the other not

	Firm A	Firm B	Consequence	ML advantage
Application of ML in big data analysis	×	✓	Data is analysed and quantified to understand the financial resources, personnel and operational and technological resources required. This informs the budgetary requirements. Mapping this data to ensure that there is life to the implementation plan is crucial for firms so that they know where to invest resources. This process could otherwise be time-consuming and full of errors if traditional methods are deployed	The disadvantage of a firm not applying ML in Big Data Analytics is the potential misalignment between the key resources required to deliver the strategy and budgetary constraints. The misalignment could lead to the failure to achieve the firm's goals. The firm deploying ML gains an advantage associated with uncovering key trends and patterns within data to provide further insights that are crucial in aligning and identifying key priorities, budgetary requirements, accountabilities and the short-term as well as the long-term priorities

Source: Authors' own illustration

Description of Step D: Securing enough budget is one of the critical elements of the implementation of a strategy. When a firm formulates a strategy, this process could put additional demand for financial resources in order to develop new processes, purchase new equipment and even recruit new employees among other initiatives. As a result, budgetary support is required to ensure that all these initiatives are properly resourced and can be implemented at the right time. In addition, both the operating and capital budgets need to be linked with each aspect of strategy.

Role of ML in Step D: This step is similar to the creation of implementation plans, as the achievement of the overarching implementation plan hinges on the identification of resources required and the steps that need to be followed to achieve the goals. Data are analysed and quantified to understand the financial resources. There could be various sources of data. The allocation of financial resources has to be guided by the firm's priorities in the short and long term. The data will be structured and unstructured. Mapping this data ensures that there is life in the implementation plan, which could otherwise be time-consuming if traditional methods are deployed. The ability of ML to handle this type of data is important for a firm to uncover key trends and patterns within data to provide further insights that are crucial in identifying key priorities and budgetary requirements in the short term and long term. In Table 5.12, we illustrate a typical example of aligning and identifying key priorities and

Table 5.13 Difference between two firms, one deploying ML for big data analysis and the other not

	Firm	Firm B	Consequence	ML advantage
Application of ML in big data analysis	×	✓	Big data will provide insights relating to the key capabilities of key individuals assigned a role within a strategy. This is important for the achievement of the desired performance	The firm applying ML in Big Data Analytics gains an advantage in the in-depth analysis of major key interdependencies between individuals driving the strategy and understanding their key capabilities. This allows the firm an opportunity to assign responsibilities accordingly. Decisions on the assignments are data-intensive and data-informed. The risk of failure to deliver on the assigned responsibility would have been carefully calibrated

Source: Authors' own illustration

budgetary requirements in the short term as well as in the long term between two firms, one deploying ML for big data analysis and the other not.

Step E: Assigning objectives and responsibilities

Description of Step E: This step requires that strategic responsibilities and objectives be assigned clearly to enable employees to better understand their roles and responsibilities within the strategy. If this is done properly, individuals are likely to take ownership of specific strategic tasks and outcomes. Everyone assigned a role to play in the implementation need to have a clear idea of the outcomes and the responsibility they hold for these outcomes to be fulfilled. The duty to ensure that all the employees understand the roles they play and how their roles contribute to the objectives of the firm rests with the senior leadership team as it formulates and monitors strategy implementation.

Role of ML in Step E: We previously indicated that the strategic choice would be a function of understanding vast sets of data, which are converted to information by ML algorithms. Similarly, the allocation of responsibilities to various individuals will be a function of understanding vast data, including capabilities and interdependencies of various key individuals driving the strategy within the firm. Additional data could include the internal and external contexts; macroeconomic factors; the industry in which the company operates; the strengths, weaknesses, opportunities, threats, interdependencies and key internal and external stakeholders; behaviour of competitors; behaviour of clients; targets; and performance measures among other key things. In Table 5.13, we illustrate a typical example of assigning responsibilities by two firms, one deploying ML for big data analysis and the other not.

Table 5.14 Difference between two firms, one deploying ML for big data analysis and the other not

	Firm A	Firm B	Consequence	ML advantage
Application of ML in big data analysis	×	✓	Big data will provide insights relating to the key processes and structures within a strategy. This is important for the achievement of the desired performance	The firm applying ML in Big Data Analytics gains an advantage in the in-depth analysis of major key interdependencies between the processes and structures driving the strategy and understanding their key capabilities. This allows the firm an opportunity to align these structures and systems accordingly. Decisions on the alignment are data-intensive and data-informed. ML provides key insights relating to the key processes and structures that contribute to the achievement of the desired performance

Source: Authors' own illustration

Step F: Alignment of structures and processes

Description of Step F: In strategy implementation, alignment of structures and processes should be a priority. In most cases, the plans, processes and structures of many firms operate in isolation and sometimes with little relationship even to firm strategy. For a firm to implement the strategy effectively, structures and processes need to be aligned with the strategic objectives. In the alignment of the structure of the firm with strategic objectives, activities should be coordinated, and the skills and capabilities of the firm should be made available for the benefit of the firm. In addition, it is important to align the ongoing and proposed projects to strategic objectives. A full assessment and evaluation of the contribution of each project towards the strategic objectives will inform decisions such as which projects should be resourced and carried through to completion.

Role of ML in Step F: Similar to the discussions above, we previously indicated that the strategic choice will be a function of understanding vast sets of data, which is converted to information by ML algorithms. In addition, the alignment of structures and processes of different segments will be a function of understanding vast data, including capabilities and interdependencies of various key segments driving the strategy within the firm. Misalignments could lead to failure of a segment to perform, which could affect other segments. We see the role of ML as the provision of key insights relating to the key processes and structures that contribute to the achievement of the desired performance. In Table 5.14, we illustrate a typical example of

Table 5.15 Difference between two firms, one deploying ML for big data analysis and the other not

	Firm A	Firm B	Consequence	ML advantage
Application of ML in big data analysis	×	✓	Big data will provide insights relating to the human capital factors that could contribute to the achievement or non-achievement of the desired performance. These factors could then be analysed to make informed decisions	The firm applying ML in Big Data Analytics gains an advantage in the analysis of internal and external environments to understand the factors driving employee performance. Decisions whether to supplement employee capabilities are data-intensive and data-informed. They are risk calibrated

Source: Authors' own illustration

alignment of structures and processes by two firms, one deploying ML for big data analysis and the other not.

Step G: Alignment of human capital

Description of Step G: Effective people management is an important issue in the successful implementation of a strategy. The contributions of all the employees of a firm should be aligned with the strategy of the firm. This alignment helps employees to align with the achievement of the firm's objectives. For the implementation to be successful, it is important that firms create a cohesive strategy that employees can understand and engage with effectively.

Role of ML in Step G: This step requires that data be analysed to understand the contribution of each team player to the desired goal. Big data will provide insights relating to the factors that could contribute to the team player failing to contribute to the achievement or non-achievement of the desired performance. The decision can then be made as to where resources need to be ploughed to improve performance or to leverage the process so that it yields even better results. Automated systems are also able to report the performance of a team player in real time. Should the senior leadership team wish to see the performance of a team player at a certain time frame, they need not wait for the performance review period. They are able to access this and correct any deviation on an ongoing basis. In Table 5.15, we illustrate a typical example of the human capital alignment by two firms, one deploying ML for big data analysis and the other not.

Step H: Communication of strategy across the firm

Description of Step H: Communication of strategic imperatives is another critical aspect of strategy implementation. All critical stakeholders, particularly the firm's employees, should understand the core elements of the strategy and the way this strategy should be executed. Communication of the strategy normally has a positive impact on productivity. In order to ensure that people understand the firm's strategy, vague statements should be avoided, and objectives should be expressed concretely

Table 5.16 Difference between two firms, one deploying ML for big data analysis and the other not

	Firm A	Firm B	Consequence	Competitive advantage
Application of ML in big data analysis	×	✓	The firm applying ML in Big Data Analytics is able to uncover key trends and patterns within data to provide further insights that are crucial in eliminating any ambiguity	The firm applying ML in Big Data Analytics gains insights that are crucial in crafting the message and strategies aimed at delivering the desired results. ML algorithms are trained to deliver insights that are crucial in eliminating any ambiguity

Source: Authors' own illustration

and measurably with results that are tangibly achievable in expected time frames. When communicating strategy, there are important issues to be considered, namely, the messages to be communicated, audience to be reached, behavioural changes needed, communication channels to be used and measures to evaluate the level of success or failure. Merely handing a copy of the strategy is rarely effective. As such, there should be a separate document that should be prepared with a summary of critical and significant points, which should be clear and concise. The other mistake that should be avoided is jargon, as the message should be simple, clear, convincing and compelling.

Role of ML in Step H: The main advantage of technology-driven tools is that they are digital. Critical points that the senior leadership needs to communicate across the group could be communicated through the digital tools. We indicated that ML could take supervised learning, unsupervised learning and reinforcement learning. The process includes data collection, data preparation, training, evaluation and tuning in all these types of learning. As algorithms receive data, they will learn and understand the data and the intended outcomes better. What is further clear is that the stored internal data comes in both structured and unstructured forms. The massive amounts of data are troublesome for traditional methods. The ability of ML to handle this type of data is important for a firm to uncover key trends and patterns within data to provide further insights that are crucial in eliminating any ambiguity. Table 5.16 illustrates a typical example of the external situational analysis of two firms, one deploying ML for big data analysis and the other not.

Step I: Reviewing and reporting on progress

Description of Step I: Reviewing progress should be done regularly to check if the strategy is being implemented as planned. This stage is critical because senior leadership can track progress, check on priorities and identify any issues that may need to be tackled. Strategy review is more to do with results than control of performance. Meetings to review the strategy should be done continuously to keep the implementation process on course and to allow the managers to take decisions on any required adjustments. Reviews can be weekly at first, then bi-weekly, then monthly and then quarterly. The frequency of the reviews needs to be scaled back

Table 5.17 Difference between two firms, one deploying ML for big data analysis and the other not

	Firm A	Firm B	Consequence	ML advantage
Application of ML in big data analysis	×	✓	Big data will provide insights relating to the factors contributing to the achievement or non-achievement of the desired performance, which is crucial to check if the strategy is delivering the envisaged results. This key matrix being tracked could then be analysed to make informed decisions	The firm applying ML in Big Data Analytics gains an advantage in the analysis of performance to understand the factors driving performance. Decisions whether to supplement the process are data-intensive and data-informed. They are risk calibrated. Furthermore, several factors influencing performance can be integrated. These factors could be vast, containing both internal and external data and structured and unstructured data. Traditional approaches would not have capabilities to track these factors, including the early warning indicators

Source: Authors' own illustration

especially when the implementation process has been established and the managers are sure that it is now working very well. The frequency of the meetings also depends on the activities undertaken. Sometimes more frequency is required when the strategy is coming up with major changes to the firm and when the business environment is evolving rapidly.

Role of ML in Step I: We indicated in step E that data are analysed to pick up the gaps between the desired and the actual goals. Big data will provide insights relating to the factors contributing to the achievement or non-achievement of the desired performance. This is important in checking whether the strategy is implemented as envisaged. A decision can then be made as to where resources need to be ploughed to improve performance or to leverage the process so that it yields even better results. Automated systems are also able to report the performance in real time. Should senior leadership wish to see performance at a certain period, they need not wait for reporting timelines. In Table 5.17, we illustrate a typical example of reviewing and reporting of performance by two firms, one deploying ML for big data analysis and the other not.

5.7 Key Points

- ML is a concept that addresses the question related to how to construct computers that are capable of improving automatically through experience.
- Over the years, ML has grown substantially. Its growth and progress could be attributed to online data availability and low-cost computation.
- Three forms of ML exist, namely, supervised learning, unsupervised learning and reinforced learning.
- Two types of learning exist, and these are deep learning (DL) and shallow learning (SL).
- SL would typically contain the single-layer neural networks, whereas DL would contain many layers of neural networks.
- DL requires more computation power for forward or backward optimisation while training, testing and eventually running these neural networks.
- DL often outperforms shallow ML methods which often consist of single neural networks.
- The firm applying ML in Big Data Analytics would gain an advantage in the variety of factors affecting strategy and strategy implementation.

References

Alpaydin, E. (2020). *Introduction to machine learning* (4th ed.). Cambridge, MA: The MIT Press.

Barpaga, P. (2019). *A gentle introduction to machine learning*. Available from: https://www.towardsdatascience.com/a-gentle-introduction-to-machine-learning-599210ec34ad

Chauhan, S., Vig, L., Grazia, M. F., Corbetta, M., Ahmad, S., & Zorzi, M. (2019). A comparison of shallow and deep learning methods for predicting cognitive performance of stroke patients from MRI lesion images. *Frontiers in Neuroinformatics, 13*(53), 1–12.

Chollet, F. (2017). *Deep learning with Python*. Shelter Island Manning.

Edwards, G. (2018). *Machine learning: An introduction*. Available from: https://www.towardsdatascience.com/machine-learning-an-introduction-23b84d51e6d0

Freiherr, G. (2019). Are shallow networks better than Deep ones? *Int. Imaging Technology News*. Available from: https://www.itonline.com/article/are-shallow-networks-better-deep-ones

Genc, O. (2019). *Notes on artificial intelligence, machine learning and deep learning for curious people*. Available from: https://www.towardsdatascience.com/notes-on-artificial-intelligence-ai-machine-learning-ml-deep-learning-dl-for-56e51a2071c2

Glose, A. (2018). *An intuitive introduction to machine learning*. Available from: https://www.becominghuman.ai/an-intuitive-introduction-to-machine-learning-57b2b1bd3d6

Jagreet, K. G. (2018). *Automatic log analysis using deep learning and AI*. Available at https://www.xenonstack.com/blog/log-analytics-deep-machine-learning/

Jordan, M. I., & Mitchell, T. M. (2015). Machine learning: Trends, perspectives, and prospects. *Science, 349*(6245), 255–260.

Keshari, K. (2020). *Top 10 applications of machine learning: Machine learning applications in daily life*. Available from: https://www.edureka.co/blog/machine-learning-applications/

Lloyd, S. (2015). *What do you think about machines that think? Edge*. Available from: https://www.edge.org/response-detail/26137

Marshall, R. (2019). AI: Deep learning vs shallow thinking. *DH Deccan Herald*. Available from: https://www.deccanherald.com/opinion/panorama/ai-deep-learning-vs-shallow-thinking-728066.html

McCulloch, W. S., & Pitts, W. H. (1943). A logical calculus of the ideas immanent in nervous activity. *The Bulletin of Mathematical Biophysics, 5*, 115–133.

Moloi, T., & Marwala, T. (2020). *Artificial intelligence in economics and finance theories*. Springer Nature, Switzerland AG.

Piekniewski, F. (2019). *Deep learning and shallow data*. Available from: https://www.blog.piekniewski.info/2019/04/07/deep-learning-and-shallow-data/

Priyadharshini. (2020). *What is machine learning and how does it work*. Available from: https://www.simplilearn.com/what-is-machine-learning-and-why-it-matters-article

Rosenblatt, F. (1961). *Perceptrons and the theory of brain mechanics*. Buffalo, NY: Cornell Aeronautical Lab.

Sejnowski, T. J. (2020). *The unreasonable effectiveness of deep learning in artificial intelligence*. Available from: https://www.pnas.org/content/pnas/early/2020/01/23/1907373117.full.pdf

Natural Language Processing in Strategy and Implementation

6

6.1 Introduction

Chapter 5 provided an overview of the concept of ML. This was followed by a discussion of the growing influence of ML. Subsequently, a discussion on the forms of ML followed. Furthermore, deep learning was briefly introduced, and the final part of the chapter explored ML in strategy and strategy implementation.

This chapter attends to natural language processing (NLP). Accordingly, the NLP started in the 1950s as a convergence of AI and linguistics (Nadkarni et al., 2011). Previously, NLP was controlled by rule-based systems originally by writing rules such as grammar and stemming. This system was time-consuming and did not work well (Heller, 2019). The limitations of hand-written rules saw the ascent of statistical inference NLP models in the 1980s and early 1990s (Nadkarni et al., 2011).

Klein (2005) indicates that the 1980s brought with them improvements in the NLP to address the limitations of the rule-based system. Improvements included replacing the simple, robust approximations with deep analysis, the introduction of evaluation that is more rigorous, the prominence of probability-based machine-learning methods and the employment of large annotated bodies of text (corpora) to train machine-learning algorithms. Heller (2019) hails this re-orientation and further argues that it gave birth to the statistical NLP, which significantly improved the rule-based systems.

This chapter discusses the concept of NLP in Sect. 6.2. This is followed by a discussion of how NLP is applied in Sect. 6.3. Section 6.4 outlines the typical functions of the NLP, and Sect. 6.5 explores the NLP in strategy and strategy implementation.

T. Moloi, T. Marwala, *Artificial Intelligence and the Changing Nature of Corporations*, Future of Business and Finance,
https://doi.org/10.1007/978-3-030-76313-8_6

6.2 Understanding Natural Language Processing

Reshamwala et al. (2013) define NLP as a branch of computer science, AI and linguistics that focuses on the interaction between computer programs and human language. Human language is also called the natural language.

For Garbade (2018), NLP is a technology used to help computers understand the natural language. Natural languages are used to express human knowledge and emotions. Human knowledge and emotions are then transmitted to other people. The transmission can occur using different forms of communication. As such, the NLP technology aims to read, decode, comprehend and make sense of human languages (Garbade, 2018).

Reshamwala et al. (2013) believe that NLP can be a valuable tool for the tutoring systems, duplicate detection, computer-supported instruction and database interface fields avenue for increased interactivity and productivity.

There has been scepticism towards the use of the NLP. However, Heller (2019) believes that the NLP is currently one of the significant prosperous application areas of deep learning. According to Heller (2019), the NLP could be used for a variety of things, including:

- Automatic summarisation
- Co-reference resolution (this is the determination of words referring to the same objects, especially for pronouns)
- Machine translation
- Named entity recognition (this could be the identification of people, places and firms)
- Natural language generation (this could be a conversion of information into readable language)
- Natural language understanding (this could be a conversion of chunks of text into more formal representations such as first-order logic structures)
- Part-of-speech tagging
- Sentiment analysis (this could be a classification of text as favourable or unfavourable toward specific objects)
- Speech recognition (this could be a conversion of audio to text) (Heller, 2019)

6.3 Applications of the Natural Language Processing

According to Reshamwala et al. (2013), there are two main applications of NLP, namely, speech recognition (SR) and speech synthesis (SS). SS is based on the text to speech conversion (TTS) in which the text data is the first input into the system. Accordingly, it uses high-level modules for speech synthesis.

There are two ways in which SS synthesises the speech. These are segmentation and tokenisation. Typically, the NLP for speech uses sentence segmentation, which deals with punctuation marks with a simple decision tree. It would then contemplate aspects usually taken when reading a text (Reshamwala et al., 2013).

According to Reshamwala et al. (2013), tokenisation refers to the process of splitting a string or words. Accordingly, tokenisation separates the units that build up a piece of text and splits the text of the sentences at white spaces and punctuation marks typically.

Concerning the SR, Schild (2016) indicates that the automatic speech recognition (ASR) system uses NLP techniques in a relatively restricted way based on grammar. Accordingly, grammar refers to a set of rules that determine the structure of texts written in a given language by defining its morphology and syntax (Schild, 2016).

Furthermore, Schild (2016) indicates that the system would typically use the context-free grammars to represent that language's syntax. It further presents a means of dealing with spontaneous language through the spotlighting addition of automatic summarisation, including indexing, which extracts the gist of the speech transcriptions to deal with information retrieval and dialogue system issues (Schild, 2016).

According to Reshamwala et al. (2013), NLP techniques are applied in ASR when modelling the language or domain of interaction in question. Accordingly, the structures for the language are defined through the production of an accurate set of grammar rules. In the view of Reshamwala et al. (2013), these rules can either be hand-crafted or derived from the statistical analyses performed on a labelled corpus of data.

6.4 Typical Functions of the NLP

As indicated before, here are three functions of the NLP, namely, machine translation (MT), summarisation and sentiment analysis (SA). These are discussed below.

6.4.1 Machine Translation

MT is a branch of computer linguistics that analyses the use of computerised tools to translate the context derived from this, from one language to the next. The language translated is the human language.

According to Nemeth (2019), MT refers to machines' tasks to convert one natural language into the other automatically. The most important thing is that while the natural language is being translated, the original meaning must be preserved.

According to Schild (2016), MT technology originated in the early twentieth century. This technology could not be regarded as a wholly realised tool until developments in the field in the 1980s and the 1990s. Schild (2016) and Nemeth (2019) indicate that the 1930s laid out the groundwork for MT. Between 1930 and 1980, there were difficulties in the field. The period between 1990 and 2000, which was primarily characterised by digitisation, saw a boom in MT research and development (Schild, 2016).

6.4.1.1 Approaches to Machine Translation

There are three major approaches in MT, namely, rule-based MT, statistical MT and neural MT (Nemeth, 2019). These are described below.

Rule-Based Machine Translation

According to Nemeth (2019), rule-based systems would typically require the expert to know both the source and the target languages. This knowledge is then used to develop syntactic, semantic and morphological rules to achieve the translation. Nemeth (2019) indicates that the rule-based system contains a pipeline of NLP tasks, including tokenisation, part-of-speech tagging and other tasks.

Statistical Machine Translation

According to Nemeth (2019), this approach uses statistical models based on the analysis of bilingual text corpora. Accordingly, the statistical machine translation requires that the following questions be answered:

- First, what is the correct word, given its context? This is a search for the language model.
- Secondly, what is the translation of a given word? This is a search for the translation model.
- Finally, what is the method to find the proper order of words? This is a search for the discovery method.

Neural Machine Translation

Schild (2016) indicates that the neural machine translation approach uses neural networks to achieve machine translation. The neural machine translation can be constructed with one network instead of a pipeline of separate tasks (Schild, 2016). Peng (2018) observes that companies such as Google and Microsoft are now using neural-based models.

The three paragraphs above discussed three significant approaches in MT, namely, the rule-based MT, statistical MT and neural MT. If the company was to adopt the MT, what advantages can be derived? What could be the disadvantages? The sections below outline the advantages and disadvantages of MT.

6.4.1.2 Advantages of Machine Translation

According to Dilmanc (n.d.), the following advantages can be derived from using MT:

- ML can enable the firm or individuals to save time while translating large volumes of texts.
- Professional translators could be costly if the idea behind the translation is to get an idea of what the text is talking about (the essence of the message). In essence, MT could be a cost-effective and helpful tool for firms and individuals.

- MT could be a useful tool to translate sensitive information that the owner of the information would not want anyone else to see. In a sense, it is a better tool to translate confidential information compared to human beings.
- Professional translators could be specialised professionals. This means that if the text to be translated is not in the specialised realm of the engaged professional translator, the firm or an individual requiring translation would have to source another translator. MT can translate any text. Therefore, it has the advantage of universality.
- MT has the advantage of being an online service. Information can be translated promptly. Any content that needs to be translated from various online databases such as websites and other search engines could easily be translated instantly.

6.4.1.3 Disadvantages of Machine Translation

According to Dilmanc (nd), as much as MT has the advantages discussed above, it also has disadvantages. The following disadvantages are noted:

- MT lacks superior exactness. This means that since MT cannot provide a firm or individual with accurate precision when it comes to the translation, it would be difficult to rely on it to translate official documents, contracts, etc.
- Some words are ambiguous. MT programs sometimes find it challenging to solve ambiguity. Professional translators can provide a firm or individual with accurate precision when it comes to translation. They are a reliable source for translation of official documents, contracts, etc.

6.4.2 Text Summarisation

According to Joshi (2018), automatic text summarisation refers to a process of bringing about a succinct and meaningful summary of the text. This could be taken from various text resources such as books, news articles, blog posts, research papers, emails, tweets, etc. It is clear from this that a summary of text could come from all sorts of data, particularly unstructured data.

According to Pai (2019), automatic text summarisation should be viewed as the task of producing a brief and articulate summary, while the overall meaning of that text should be maintained. Joshi (2018) indicates that automatic text summarisation was not as popular at its inception. Even though it came into existence in the 1950s, it has only recently gained a huge prominence because of the availability of large amounts of textual data. The availability of a large amount of textual data and these machines' ability to summarise it promptly have plunged the automatic summarisation system into spotlight (Garbade, 2018).

As summarisation gains prominence, supported by the ever-increasing amount of data circulating in the digital space, ML algorithms can automatically shorten longer texts and produce succinct summaries to convey the intended messages succinctly (Mayo, 2019). According to Joshi (2018), there are two broad categories of text summarisation, namely, extractive summarisation and abstractive summarisation. These two broad approaches are discussed below.

6.4.2.1 Extractive Summarisation

According to Joshi (2018) and Pai (2019), the extractive summarisation method identifies the original text's main sentences or phrases. After that, the method will then extract and stack these together to create a summary (Pai, 2019).

According to Mayo (2019), text summarisation in the NLP is treated as a supervised machine learning problem. This is where future outcomes are predicted based on provided data. The following steps illustrate how the extraction-based summarisation works:

- Step 1 introduces a method to extract the merited key phrases from the source document.
- Step 2 includes the gathering of text documents with positively labelled key phrases. The most important aspect of this step is that the key phrases should be compatible to the stipulated extraction technique, and negatively labelled key phrases can also be created to increase accuracy.
- Step 3 includes training a binary ML classifier to make the text summarisation. Mayo (2019) advises that some of the features that can be used include the length of the key phrase, its frequency, the most recurring word in the key phrase and the number of characters in the key phrase.
- Step 4 includes the creation and classification of all the key phrase words and sentences (Mayo, 2019).

Pai (2019) warns that it is important to identify the right sentences for the extractive summarisation method to work as intended. Figure 6.1 illustrates how extractive summarisation works.

An example of extractive summarisation could be as follows:

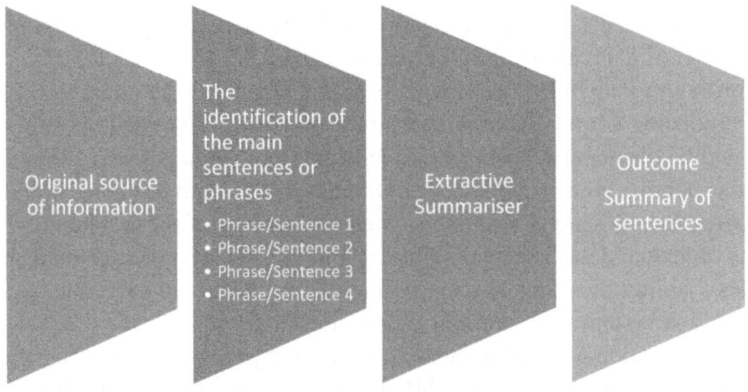

Fig. 6.1 Typical extractive summarisation. Source: Authors' own illustration, with information obtained from Joshi (2018) and Pai (2019)

The Business Times reports that in 2021, the global economy will contract by 5% because of the pandemic which has impacted the supply chain lines and general travelling by business executives.

In our example above:

The original source of information: the Business Times
Main sentences/phrases:
Sentence 1: The global economy will contract by 5% in 2021.
Sentence 2: The pandemic is impacting the global supply chain lines.
Sentence 3: The pandemic is impacting global travels by executives of firms.
Extractive summary could be: The global economy will decline by 5% due to the pandemic which has impacted the supply chain lines and travelling.

6.4.2.2 Abstractive Summarisation

According to Pai (2019), the abstractive summarisation method involves paraphrasing parts of the source text. It uses advanced NLP techniques to generate new sentences from the original text to produce a summary. Notably, some parts of this summary may not even be found in the original text. According to Mayo (2019), abstractive methods use more powerful language processing techniques to interpret text and develop new summary text, unlike the extractive methods that select the most representative existing excerpts to perform summarisation.

The application of abstraction for text summarisation in deep learning problems helps overcome the grammar inconsistencies that are exhibited by the extractive method; hence, abstraction performs better than extraction (Garbade, 2018). Furthermore, Garbade (2018) highlights the difficulty in developing the text summarisation algorithms required to do abstraction, thus making the use of extraction popular. Figure 6.2 illustrates how extractive summarisation works.

Using our example above to illustrate the abstractive summarisation, we state:

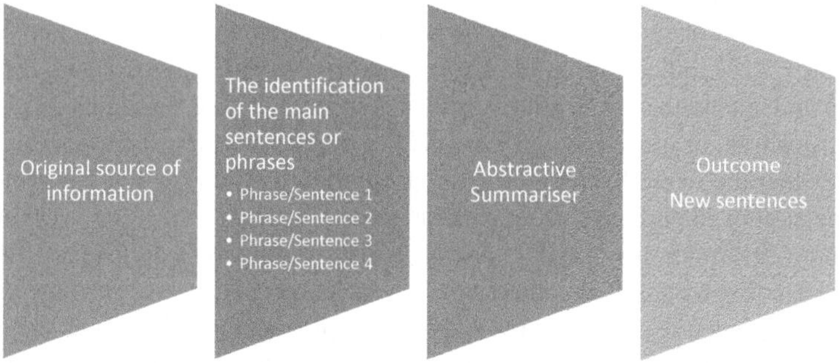

Fig. 6.2 Typical abstractive summarisation. Source: Authors' own illustration, with information obtained from Joshi (2018) and Pai (2019)

The Business Times reports that in 2021, the global economy will contract by 5% because of the pandemic which has impacted the supply chain lines and general travelling by business executives.

In our example above:

The original source of information: the Business Times
Main sentences/phrases:
Sentence 1: The global economy will contract by 5% in 2021.
Sentence 2: The pandemic is impacting the global supply chain lines.
Sentence 3: The pandemic is impacting the global travels by executives of firms.
Abstractive summary could be: The global economy is expected to decline by 5% in 2021 because the pandemic has restricted supply chain lines and travelling.

6.4.3 Sentiment Analysis

Sentiment analysis (SA) is often called opinion mining. Godbole et al. (2007) view SA as a way of finding out the polarity or strength of the opinion (e.g. positive or negative) that is expressed in written text. According to Taj et al. (2019), SA models focus on polarity of emotions. They could be positive, negative or neutral. SA also focuses on feelings and emotions. A human can have a feeling or emotion of anger, happiness or sadness. Furthermore, SA can even focus on intentions, for instance, humans could either be interested or not interested.

MonkeyLearn (2020) defines SA as the interpretation and classification of emotions (positive, negative and neutral) within text data in either the document as a whole, the paragraph as a whole, a sentence as a whole or the clause. The interpretation and classification of either negative, positive or neutral emotions within the original text data uses the text analysis techniques.

According to Rajput (2019), the sentiment analysis field utilises techniques from NLP. The techniques from NLP would look at users' expressions and associate emotions with what the user has provided. Therefore, Rajput (2019) advises that the basic application of sentiment analysis lies in gathering the opinion of people.

Sarkar (2018) indicates that the key aspect of SA is to analyse a body of text in order to understand the opinion it expresses. Accordingly, the sentiment is quantified with a positive or negative value, called polarity. Furthermore, Sarkar (2018) indicates that the overall sentiment is often inferred as positive, neutral or negative from the sign of the polarity score (Sarkar, 2018).

Rajput (2019) submits that the SA works best on text with a subjective context as compared to text with only an objective context. This is because, according to Rajput (2019), the objective text has a disadvantage of generally depicting the normal statements or facts without the human expressing any emotion, feelings or mood, whereas the subjective text contains text generally expressed by a human with typical moods, emotions and feelings.

According to Taj et al. (2019), SA has become one of the widely used methods in social media analysis. Most businesses would use SA to, for instance, gauge a mood on a recent movie, a recent product launch, etc. This assists in understanding the reception of a product or service by the people. It also assists in gauging what people think of a new product (Taj et al., 2019).

In this regard, Taj et al. (2019) argues that SA has become an important tool for firms to make sense of the world's abundant unstructured text data. The unstructured text data could be in the in the form of emails, support tickets, chats, social media conversations, surveys, articles and documents (Taj et al., 2019). The unstructured text data of this nature is created on a daily basis. Without tools such as the SA, it will be difficult and time-consuming to analyse, understand and sort through it.

According to MonkeyLearn (2020), there are four popular types of SA, namely, the fine-grained SA, emotion detection, aspect-based SA and multilingual SA. These are described below:

- The fine-grained sentiment analysis—Firms can improve polarity precision by expanding the polarity categories. MonkeyLearn (2020) advises that this could include categories such as Very positive, Positive, Neutral, Negative and Very negative (MonkeyLearn, 2020).
- Emotion detection—This type of SA focuses on detecting emotions like happiness, frustration, anger and sadness among human emotions. MonkeyLearn (2020) points out that most emotion detection systems use what is called lexicons. Lexicons are lists of words and the emotions they convey. They could also use complex machine learning algorithms (MonkeyLearn, 2020).
- Multilingual sentiment analysis—This type of SA is one of the difficult forms of analysis. It would typically involve a lot of pre-processing. These resources, such as sentiment lexicons, would mostly be available online. Other resources such as translated corpora or noise detection algorithms would need to be created.
- The aspect-based SA—This SA is applied when analysing sentiments of texts such as in product reviews to establish which particular aspects or features people are mentioning in a positive, neutral or negative way (MonkeyLearn, 2020).

6.5 Natural Language Processing in Strategy and Strategy Implementation

The concept of strategy was discussed in detail in Chap. 3, where it was indicated that from a business perspective, strategy refers to a way in which firms explain to their stakeholders the ways the firm would be moving forward. Accordingly, it was indicated that firm strategy is generally viewed as a course of action that can help the firm in attaining its objectives. There are three aspects of strategy formulation, namely:

- The corporate-level strategy
- The competitive strategy (sometimes called the business strategy)
- The parenting strategy

Chapter 3 emphasised that the growth or directional strategy outlines the growth objective of the firm, particularly on how to achieve this. A point was raised that the portfolio strategy outlines the portfolio of the lines of the firm, which assist in the diversification that the business should engage in. The parenting strategy was said to explain how resources are allocated and managed, especially on areas on which to put more emphasis.

Chapter 3 also indicated that strategy contains three phases, namely, the diagnosis, formulation and implementation. This section explores the role of NLP in traditional business processes such as strategy and strategy implementation. It explores the role of NLP in the diagnosis, formulation and implementation phases.

6.5.1 Exploring the Role of NLP and ML in a Typical Strategy Diagnosis Process

Step A: Situational analysis of internal environment

Description of Step A: Diagnosis involves carrying out a situation analysis where the firm's internal environment is analysed, including identifying and evaluating the current mission, strategic objectives, strategies and results and significant strengths and weaknesses.

Role of NLP and ML in Step A: The situation analysis would require that a firm process the stored internal data to extract value from it. The massive volume of spoken data required to evaluate and inform the mission, strategic objectives, strategies and strengths and weaknesses of a firm would typically be complex if it were to be done manually and by a human being. The NLP has two main applications, namely, speech recognition (SR) and speech synthesis (SS). Once the algorithms are trained to recognise a particular language or once they synthesise it, then it can be exported to the ML. It is clear here that as the ML algorithms receive data exported from the NLP, they will better understand the firm. What is further clear is that the stored internal data comes in both structured and unstructured ways. These massive amounts of data are troublesome for traditional methods. The ability of ML to handle this type of data is important for a firm to uncover key trends and patterns within data to provide further insights that are crucial for crafting the mission, strategic objectives, strategies and desired results and significant strengths and weaknesses. Table 6.1 illustrates a typical example of the external situational analysis of two firms, one deploying NLP and ML for big data analysis and the other not.

Step B: Situational analysis of the external environment

Description of Step B: Strategy diagnosis further involves analysing the firm's external environment, which comprises opportunities and threats. It also involves analysing the firm's external environment, which also includes major opportunities

Table 6.1 Difference between two firms, one deploying NLP and ML for big data analysis and the other not

	Firm A	Firm B	Consequence	Competitive advantage
Application of NLP and ML in big data analysis	×	✓	The firm applying NLP and ML in Big Data Analytics can uncover critical trends and patterns within data	The firm applying NLP and ML in Big Data Analytics gains insights crucial for crafting the mission, strategic objectives, strategies, desired results and significant strengths and weaknesses facing the firm

Source: Authors' own illustration

and threats. Lastly, diagnosis involves identifying the critical issues, which are sometimes two to five of the major problems, threats, weaknesses and opportunities that demand high priority and attention.

Role of NLP and ML in Step B: The situation analysis would require that a firm process the available external data to extract value from it. This data could come from industry sources, national and international statistical agencies, business news, securities exchange, news services, experts' opinions, etc. This could come in the form of spoken language, i.e. interviews. The speech recognition (SR) and speech synthesis (SS) could then be deployed to extract, recognise or synthesise this data. Once the algorithms are trained to recognise a particular language or to synthesise it, then it can be exported to the ML. The massive volume of data required to evaluate and inform the mission, strategic objectives, strategies and major opportunities and threats of a firm would typically be complex if it were to be done manually and by a human being. As explained earlier, ML can take supervised learning, unsupervised learning and reinforcement learning forms. The typical process includes data collection, data preparation, training, evaluation and tuning in all these types of learning. It is clear here that as algorithms receive data, they will learn and understand the firm better. What is further clear is that the stored internal data comes in both structured and unstructured ways. These massive amounts of data are troublesome and very time-consuming if traditional methods are deployed. The ability of ML to handle this type of data is important for a firm to uncover key trends and patterns within data to provide further insights that are crucial for crafting the mission, strategic objectives, strategies and desired results and significant opportunities and threats. Table 6.2 illustrates a typical example of the external situational analysis of two firms, one deploying NLP and ML for big data analysis and the other not.

6.5.2 Exploring the Role of NLP and ML in a Typical Strategy Formulation Process

Step A: Objective setting

Table 6.2 Difference between two firms, one deploying NLP and ML for big data analysis and the other not

	Firm A	Firm B	Consequence	ML advantage
Application of NLP and ML in big data analysis	×	✓	The firm applying NLP and ML in Big Data Analytics can uncover key trends and patterns within external data	The firm applying NLP and ML in Big Data Analytics gains insights that are crucial for crafting the mission, strategic objectives, strategies, desired results and significant opportunities and threats facing the firm

Source: Authors' own illustration

Description of Step A: Analysis of each factor that influences the selection of objectives

Role of NLP and ML in Step A: The analysis of each factor that influences the selection of objectives will be a cumbersome process for traditional methods that have previously relied on human beings. There could potentially be numerous factors influencing the selection of objectives. The selection of objectives could happen in a boardroom where various factors are evaluated and considered. Each of the factors put forward has to be assessed, analysed and considered for a decision to be taken. This involves lots of spoken language. The speech recognition (SR) and speech synthesis (SS) could then be deployed to extract, recognise or synthesise this data. Once the algorithms are trained to recognise a particular language or to synthesise it, then it can be exported to the ML. ML is wired to deal with these many datasets to formulate potential scenarios that could then be analysed and the best option chosen. Objectives emanating from data-intensive and data-informed processes are risk calibrated, as several factors influencing the selection of objectives would have been considered. In Table 6.3, we illustrate a typical example of the objective setting of two firms, one deploying NLP and ML for big data analysis and the other not.

Step B: Internal and external contexts

Description of Step B: This step involves analysis of general economic and industrial environment in which the firm operates. It also involves analysis of the competition and its movement and analysis of strengths, weaknesses, threats and opportunities.

Role of ML in Step B: As noted earlier, ML is wired to deal with big data, which would otherwise be a cumbersome process for a human being or traditional methods. The analysis of general economic and industrial environments in which the firm operates, the competition and its movement as well as the firm's strengths, weaknesses, threats and opportunities could come from industry experts, in the form of a human language. Speech recognition (SR) and speech synthesis (SS) could then be deployed to extract, recognise or synthesise this data. Once the algorithms are trained to recognise a particular language or to synthesise it, then it

Table 6.3 Difference between two firms, one deploying NLP and ML for big data analysis and the other not

	Firm A	Firm B	Consequence	ML advantage
Application of NLP and ML in big data analysis	×	✓	There are potentially various factors influencing the selection of objectives by each firm. This could be time-consuming if done manually as each of them has to be assessed, analysed and considered for a decision to be taken. ML is wired to deal with the formulation of potential scenarios, which could then be analysed and the best option chosen	The firm applying NLP and ML in Big Data Analytics gains an advantage, as objectives emanating from a data-intensive and data-informed process are risk calibrated. Furthermore, several factors influencing the selection of objectives would have been considered

Source: Authors' own illustration

Table 6.4 Difference between two firms, one deploying NLP and ML for big data analysis and the other not

	Firm A	Firm B	Consequence	ML advantage
Application of NLP and ML in big data analysis	×	✓	Since the analysis of general economic and industrial environments in which the firm operates, the competition and its movement is a cumbersome process, NLP and ML provide a powerful tool for the analysis of structured and unstructured data in order for the firm to properly gauge it strengths, weaknesses, threats and opportunities properly. This requires massive data handling, labelling and integration. ML is capable of doing this and the formulation of potential scenarios	The firm applying NLP and ML in Big Data Analytics gains an advantage in the analysis of internal and external environments. The strengths, weaknesses, threats and opportunities emanate from a data-intensive and data-informed process and are therefore risk calibrated. Furthermore, factors influencing the selection of objectives are based on the properly formulated scenarios

Source: Authors' own illustration

can be exported to the ML. The abilities of ML to handle massive data are important for a firm to uncover key trends and patterns within data, which is important for insights into data. These insights are crucial in assisting a firm in formulating potential scenarios. In Table 6.4, we illustrate a typical example of the consideration

Table 6.5 Difference between two firms, one deploying NLP and ML for big data analysis and the other not

	Firm A	Firm B	Consequence	ML advantage
Application of NLP and ML in big data analysis	×	✓	A firm deploying NLP and ML will have a better idea of needs of the key stakeholders. It will also have better calibrated data for understanding both internal and external stakeholders. These are all crucial aspects in target setting	The firm applying NLP and ML, specifically a tool such as the ML user modelling platforms, could mine key stakeholder data, which could subsequently allow a firm to make an intelligent and informed decision

Source: Authors' own illustration

of external and internal environments by two firms, one deploying NLP and ML for big data analysis and the other not.

Step C: Target setting

Description of Step C: Setting the target against each stated objective

Role of ML in Step C: Setting targets requires that the firm understand its key stakeholders' needs. There is need for a firm to lend an ear to these needs, particularly when it comes to external stakeholders such as customers or investors as needs can be expressed in investor conferences, annual conferences or customer service platforms using a spoken language. We previously indicated that each objective is translated into goals that subsequently address the firm's key stakeholder needs. External stakeholders such as customers also need to be understood, specifically in relation to what product they are leaning towards, what informs such a view and what does that mean for a firm. Speech recognition (SR) and speech synthesis (SS) could then be deployed to extract, recognise or synthesise this data if it is in a natural language. Once the algorithms are trained to recognise a particular language or to synthesise it, then it can be exported to the ML. The ML user modelling platforms could be used to mine data of this nature, allowing a firm to make an informed decision. In Table 6.5, we illustrate a typical example of the targets set by two firms, one deploying NLP and ML for big data analysis and the other not.

Step D: Performance review

Description of Step D: Performance is reviewed in order to understand the gap between the actual and the planned or desired performance. This requires the analysis of past performances and projections for the future.

Role of ML in Step D: Market commentators would provide an in-depth analysis of the firm's performance against the desired targets. In most cases, the senior leadership team presents the results to the shareholders. These presentations are in a natural language format. Sometimes questions are raised, and answers are provided, all in a natural language. This step requires that data be analysed to pick up the gaps between the desired and the actual goals. Big data will provide insights relating to the factors that have contributed to the achievement or non-achievement of the desired performance. The decision can then be made as to where resources

Table 6.6 Difference between two firms, one deploying NLP and ML for big data analysis and the other not

	Firm A	Firm B	Consequence	ML advantage
Application of NLP and ML in big data analysis	×	✓	Big data will provide insights relating to the factors that have contributed to the achievement or non-achievement of the desired performance. These factors could then be analysed to make informed decisions	The firm applying NLP and ML in Big Data Analytics gains an advantage in analysing internal and external environments to understand factors driving performance. Decisions whether to supplement the process are data-intensive and data-informed. They are also risk calibrated. Furthermore, factors that influence the selection of performance are vast, containing both internal and external data and structured and unstructured data

Source: Authors' own illustration

need to be ploughed to improve performance or to leverage the process to yield even better results. Speech recognition (SR) and speech synthesis (SS) could then be deployed to extract, recognise or synthesise this data if it is in a natural language. In addition, once the algorithms are trained to recognise a particular language or to synthesise it, then it can be exported to ML. In Table 6.6, we illustrate a typical example of analysing the performance by two firms, one deploying NLP and ML for big data analysis and the other not.

Step E: Strategic choice

Description of Step E: Following the analysis of various options, the firm will make a strategic choice after having understood its strengths, weaknesses, threats and opportunities.

Role of NLP and ML in Step E: The strategic choice will help understand a vast set of data, which is converted to information by ML algorithms. This includes the internal and external contexts; macroeconomic factors; the industry in which the company operates; the strengths, weaknesses, opportunities, threats and interdependencies; the key internal and external stakeholders; behaviour of competitors; behaviour of clients; targets; and performance measures among other key factors. Some of this key information is provided in a natural language by market commentators, analysts, investors and financial institutions. Speech recognition (SR) and speech synthesis (SS) could then be deployed to extract, recognise or synthesise this data if it is in a natural language. In addition, once the algorithms are trained to recognise or synthesise a particular language, then it can be exported to the ML. In Table 6.7, we illustrate a typical example of constructing a strategic choice by two firms, one deploying NLP and ML for big data analysis and the other not.

Table 6.7 Difference between two firms, one deploying NLP and ML for big data analysis and the other not

	Firm A	Firm B	Consequence	ML advantage
Application of NLP and ML in big data analysis	×	✓	Big data will provide insights relating to the key factors driving the strategic choice to achieve the desired performance	The firm applying NLP and ML in Big Data Analytics gains an advantage in the in-depth analysis of major key factors driving the strategy choice followed. Decisions on the strategic choice are data-intensive and data-informed. The risks of the choice have been carefully calibrated

Source: Authors' own illustration

6.5.3 Exploring the Role of NLP and ML in a Typical Strategy Implementation Process

Step A: Communication of strategy across the firm

Description of Step A: Communication of strategic imperatives is another critical aspect of strategy implementation. All critical stakeholders, particularly the firm's employees, should understand the core elements of the strategy and how this strategy should be executed. Communication of the strategy normally has a positive impact on productivity. To ensure that people understand the firm's strategy, vague statements should be avoided, and objectives should be expressed concretely and measurably with tangible results in expected time frames. When communicating the strategy, there are important issues to be considered; these include the messages to be communicated, audience to be reached, behavioural changes needed, communication channels to be used and measures to evaluate the level of success or failure. Merely handing a copy of the strategy is rarely effective. There should be a separate document prepared with a summary of critical and significant points that are clear and concise. The other mistake that should be avoided is jargon, as the message should be simple, clear, convincing and compelling.

Role of ML in Step A: Communication could take the verbal or written form. Sometimes firms will use verbal communication, for instance, in executive committee meetings, team meetings, general meetings or meetings with shareholders. The main advantage of the technology-driven tools is that they are digital. Critical points that the senior leadership needs to communicate across the group could still be communicated verbally but captured through the digital tools. Communication from external stakeholders could be done verbally but captured through digital tools. Speech recognition (SR) and speech synthesis (SS) could then be deployed to extract, recognise or synthesise this data if it is in a natural language. Once the algorithms are trained to recognise a particular language or synthesise it, then it can be exported to the ML. We indicated earlier that ML could take supervised learning,

Table 6.8 Difference between two firms, one deploying NLP and ML for big data analysis and the other not

	Firm A	Firm B	Consequence	Competitive advantage
Application of NLP and ML in big data analysis	×	✓	The firm applying NLP and ML in Big Data Analytics is able to uncover key trends and patterns within data to provide further insights that are crucial in eliminating any ambiguity	The firm applying NLP and ML in Big Data Analytics gains insights that are crucial to crafting the message and strategies aimed at delivering the desired results. ML algorithms are trained to deliver insights that are crucial in eliminating any ambiguity

Source: Authors' own illustration

unsupervised learning and reinforcement learning form. The process includes data collection, data preparation, training, evaluation and tuning in all the types of learning. As algorithms receive data, they will learn and understand the data and the intended outcomes better. Further evidence shows that the stored internal data comes in both structured and unstructured ways. These massive amounts of data are troublesome for traditional methods. The abilities of ML to handle this type of data are essential for a firm to uncover key trends and patterns within data to provide further insights that are crucial in eliminating any ambiguity. Table 6.8 illustrates a typical example of communicating strategy in two firms, one deploying ML for extensive data analysis and the other not.

6.6 Key Points

- NLP is a branch of computer science, AI and linguistics that focuses on the interaction between computer programs and human language.
- There are three functions of the NLP, namely, machine translation (MT), text summarisation and sentiment analysis (SA).
- MT is a branch of computer linguistics that analyses the use of computerised tools so that it can translate the context derived from this, from one language to the next. The language that is being translated is the human language.
- Automatic text summarisation refers to a process of bringing about a succinct and meaningful summary of the text.
- SA is a way of finding out the polarity or strength of the opinion that is expressed in written text. The opinion could be positive, negative or neutral.
- MT has three significant approaches, namely, rule-based MT, statistical MT and neural MT.
- A rule-based system would typically require the expert to know both the source and target languages. This knowledge is then used to develop syntactic, semantic

and morphological rules to achieve the translation. The statistical approach uses statistical models based on the analysis of bilingual text corpora. The neural MT approach uses neural networks to achieve machine translation.
- There are two broad categories of text summarisation approaches, namely, extractive and abstractive summarisation.
- There are four popular types of SA, namely, the fine-grained SA, emotion detection, aspect-based SA and multilingual SA.
- Firms applying NLP and ML in Big Data Analytics gain better and crucial insights, setting them apart from their competitors.

References

Dilmanc. (n.d.) *Advantages and disadvantages of machine translation*. Available from http://dilmanc.az/en/technology/mtadvantages

Garbade, M. J. (2018). *A simple introduction to natural language processing*. Available from https://wwwbecominghuman.ai/a-simple-introduction-to-natural-language-processing-ea66a1747b32

Godbole, N., Srinivasaiah, M., & Skiena, S. (2007). *Large-scale sentiment analysis for news and blogs*. In International conference on weblogs and social media, Denver, CO, 2007. https://icwsm.org/papers/3%2D%2DGodbole-Srinivasaiah-Skiena.pdf

Heller, M. (2019). *What is natural language processing? AI for speech and text*. Available from https://www.infoworld.com/article/3398696/what-si-natural-language-processing-ai-for-speech-and-text.html

Joshi, P. (2018). *An introduction to text summarisation using the TextRank algorithm (with Python implementation)*. Available from https://www.analyticsvidhya.com/blog/2018/11/introduction-text-summarisation-textrank-python/

Klein, D. C. S. (2005). *Statistical natural language processing*. Available from https://www.cs.berkeley.edu-klein/cs294-5

Mayo, M. (2019). *Approaches to text summarisation: An overview*. Available from https://www.kdnuggets.com/2019/01/approaches-text-summarisation-overview.html

MonkeyLearn. (2020). *Sentiment analysis*. Available from https://www.monkeylearn.com/sentiment-analysis/

Nadkarni, P. M., Machado, L. O., & Chapman, W. W. (2011). Natural language processing: An introduction. *Journal of the American Medical Informatics Association, 18*(5), 544–551.

Nemeth, G. D. (2019). *Machine translation: A short overview*. Available from https://www.towardsdatascience.com/machine-translation-a-short-overview-91343ff39c9f

Pai, A. (2019). *Comprehensive guide to text summarisation using deep learning in Python*. Available from https://www.analyticsvidhya.com/blog/2019/06/comprehensive-guide-text-summarisation-using-deep-learning-python/

Peng, H. (2018). The impact of machine translation and computer-aided translation on translators. In IOP Conference. Series: Materials Science and Engineering, 322 (2018) 052024, IOP Publishing. Available from https://www.iopscience.iop.org/article/10.1088/1757-899X/322/5/052024/pdf

Rajput, A. (2019). *Natural language processing, sentiment analysis and clinical analytics*. Available from https://www.arxiv.org/ftp/arxiv/papers/1902/1902.00679.pdf

Reshamwala, A., Pawar, P., & Mishra, D. (2013). Review on natural language processing. *Engineering Science and Technology: An International Journal, 3*(1), 113–116.

Sarkar, D. 2018. *Emotion and sentiment analysis: A practitioner's guide to NLP*. Available from https://www.kdnuggets.com/2018/08/emotion-and-sentiment-analysis-practitioners-guide-nlp-5.html

Schild, J. (2016). *Making the most of machine translation*. Available from https://multilingual.com/making-machine-translation/?gclid=CjwKCAjwqJ_1BRBZEiwAv73uwJOmoIQvG_prcsNt2WwAqNGnJLZwc3cndQ2mD-6BazGabgLfyMPW3RoCja4QAvD_BwE

Taj, S., Shaikh, B. B., & Meghji, A. F. (2019). Sentiment analysis of news articles: A Lexicon based approach. In 2019 International conference on computing, mathematics and engineering technologies – iCOMET 2019. Available from https://www.researchgate.net/publication/330880816_Sentiment_Analysis_of_News_Articles_A_Lexicon_based_Approach

Robotic Process Automation in Strategy and Strategy Implementation

7

7.1 Introduction

Chapter 6 discussed the concept of NLP. This discussion was followed by a discussion of how the NLP is applied. The chapter further outlined typical functions of the NLP. It ended by exploring the NLP in strategy and strategy implementation.

This chapter attends to robotic process automation (RPA). According to Granta (2017), the main difference between robotics and automation is found in the fact that robots can be seen as a piece of equipment that can perform a variety of tasks when programmed. Automation is a term used for special purpose machines or systems that are designed to perform a specific task. However, Granta (2017) adds that robotics is just one of many methods of automation.

Owen-Hill (2017) argues that the difference between automation and robotics lies in their definitions. Automation can be explained as meaning the use of computer software, machines or other technologies to carry out a task that a human worker would otherwise do (Owen-Hill, 2017).

This chapter begins with a discussion of the concept of robotics in Sect. 7.2. This is followed by a discussion of the RPA in Sect. 7.3. The benefits of the RPA are also outlined in this section. Section 7.4 explores the RPA in strategy and strategy implementation.

7.2 The Difference Between Robotics and Robotic Process Automation

Robotics and RPA concepts are often confused. The confusion that occurs may be caused by the fact that there are some crossovers between robotics and RPA. According to Owen-Hill (2017), robots are used to automate physical tasks, such as in manufacturing. It is important to note that many types of automation have nothing to do with physical robots. Similarly, many branches of robotics have

T. Moloi, T. Marwala, *Artificial Intelligence and the Changing Nature of Corporations*, Future of Business and Finance,
https://doi.org/10.1007/978-3-030-76313-8_7

nothing to do with automation (Owen-Hill, 2017). In this section, we briefly provide an overview of robotics. According to Owen-Hill (2017), robotics is a branch of engineering that incorporates multiple disciplines to design, build, program and use robotic machines.

Brooks (1991) indicates that robotics is the intersection of science, engineering and technology that produces robots. Robots are often used to substitute or replicate human actions. Robotics technology has grown over a while. It is expected that as technology progresses, robotics will be reconsidered.

In line with the progression of technology, Kober et al. (2013) note that in 2005, about 90% of all robots were used to assemble cars in the automotive industry. The robots found in the automotive industry typically consist mechanical arms. These arms are used to weld or screw certain parts of a car (Kober et al., 2013; Koren & Koren, 1985).

Nof (1999) and Taylor et al. (2016) indicate that robots are an evolving phenomena, having evolved significantly over time. Nowadays, science has created bots that explore the harshest terrain in space, earth or oceans. In addition, science has created robots that assist law enforcement and healthcare professionals (Nof, 1999; Taylor et al., 2016). Furthermore, robots can perform tasks that humans could not dream of achieving (Howe & Matsuoka, 1999; Wiens et al., 2017; Williford et al., 2018).

According to Brooks (1991), Yoshikawa (1990) and Howe and Matsuoka (1999), even though there is no doubt that the world of robotics is expanding, robots have trained some consistent characteristics. These are:

- Robots would typically consist of a certain form of mechanical aspect. This is the aspect of a robot that helps it complete tasks in the environment for which it is designed. To explain this, Wiens et al. (2017) and Williford et al. (2018) note the mechanical aspect of the Mars 2020 Rover as an example. Mars Rover 2020 contains wheels that are individually motorised. Accordingly, these wheels are made of titanium tubing. The importance of this aspect is that it assists the Mars 2020 Rover to use its wheels for gripping tightly in harsh terrain such as those found in Mars.
- Robots would typically need electrical components that control and power the machinery. Accordingly, an electric current, like a battery, would be needed to power a large majority of robots (Brooks, 1991; Howe & Matsuoka, 1999; Yoshikawa, 1990).
- Robots would typically contain at least some level of computer programming. Brooks (1991), Yoshikawa (1990) and Howe and Matsuoka (1999) argue that a robot would be another piece of simple machinery without a set of codes telling it what to do. Building a program into a robot gives it the ability to know when and how to carry out a task (Brooks, 1991; Howe & Matsuoka, 1999; Yoshikawa, 1990).

7.3 Robotic Process Automation

PWC South Africa (2020) defines RPA as intelligent software to efficiently carry out manual, repeatable and time-consuming tasks that people typically perform. According to Boulton (2018), RPA is an application of technology governed by business logic and structured inputs. It aims to automate business processes. Accordingly, Boulton (2018) indicates that the RPA can be viewed as bringing together business models, strategy, process, data, humans and robots. This is done in order to achieve efficiencies within the business processes.

According to Anagnoste (2017), the RPA is the technology that permits the user to configure the computer software of a robot. Once configured, the computer software of a robot emulates and integrates human interactions within digital systems to execute a business process.

According to van der Aalst et al. (2018), the RPA process utilises the user interface to capture data and manipulate applications, in a way that human beings will. For Boulton (2018), firms can use RPA tools to configure software or a robot to do the following:

- Configured software, a robot could be used to capture and interpret applications for processing a transaction
- Configured software, a robot could be used to manipulate data
- Configured software, a robot could be used to trigger certain responses
- Configured software, a robot could be used to communicate with other digital systems (Boulton, 2018)

Several benefits can be realised from using the RPA process. According to Boulton (2018) and PWC South Africa (2020), firms can deploy RPA to realise benefits such as:

- Cost reduction—The RPA technology, on average, would cost approximately 1/3 of the cost of using an outsourced employee. This comparison yields 10% if an onsite employee was to be used.
- Time—Using the RPA reduces the process time by up to 90%.
- Better accuracy—RPA processes have better accuracy. The rate of errors declines to almost zero.
- Governance environment—The RPA improves the risk and control environment within the firm. This is critical in an environment that requires compliance
- Customer advocacy and retention—RPA improves and further strengthens customer advocacy and retention. These are some of the key factors in revenue generation.
- Improved checks and balances—The deployment of RPA frees human capital to focus on other critical aspects of the firm which they may be better at.
- Increased speed and productivity—The freeing of human capital to focus on other critical aspects of the firm, such as data interpretation, decision-making support,

customer service and business development would increase the speed of doing things and productivity.

- Integration of technologies—The RPA software is by its nature a non-intrusive technology. This means that it does not require an overhaul of the firm's legacy system. It can easily be integrated into a firm's business applications already in use.
- Super-scalable—The ability of the RPA software to easily integrate into a firm's business applications already in use means that it can perform a massive amount of operations parallel to desktop and cloud environment in use.

7.4 Robotic Process Automations in Strategy and Strategy Implementation

The concept of strategy was discussed in Chap. 3. From the business perspective, it was indicated that strategy refers to a way in which firms explain to their stakeholders how they will be moving forward. Accordingly, it was indicated that the firm strategy is generally viewed as a course of action that can help the firm in attaining its objectives. There are three aspects of strategy formulation. These are:

- The corporate-level strategy
- The competitive strategy (sometimes called the business strategy)
- The parenting strategy

Chapter 3 emphasised that the growth or directional strategy outlines the growth objective of the firm, especially on how to achieve this. A point was made that the portfolio strategy outlines the portfolio of the lines of the firm, which assist in the diversification that the business should engage in. The parenting strategy was said to explain how resources are allocated and managed especially on areas on which to put more emphasis.

Chapter 3 indicated that strategy contains three phases, namely, diagnosis, formulation and implementation. This section explores the role of RPA in traditional business processes such as strategy and strategy implementation. It explores the role of RPA in the diagnosis, formulation and implementation phases.

7.4.1 Exploring the Role of RPA in a Typical Strategy Implementation Process

Step A: Assigning objectives and responsibilities

Description of Step A: This step requires that strategic responsibilities and objectives should be assigned clearly to enable employees to better understand their roles and responsibilities within the strategy. If this is done properly, individuals are likely to take ownership of specific strategic tasks and outcomes. Everyone assigned a role to play in the implementation need to have a clear idea of

Table 7.1 Difference between two firms, one deploying RPA for automating processes and the other not

	Firm A	Firm B	Consequence	Competitive advantage
Application of RPA in key strategic processes	×	✓	The firm applying RPA in key strategic processes will be able to able to track performance in an integrated manner and across the key strategic responsibilities and objectives assigned to relevant employees	The firm applying RPA gains advantage as the performance tracking occurs on an ongoing basis, timely and free of human intervention. Those charged with governance are able to harness this information and respond timely should the need arise to ensure that the strategic responsibilities and objectives assigned to relevant employees are on track

Source: Authors' own illustration

the outcomes and the responsibilities they hold for these outcomes to be fulfilled. The duty to ensure that all the employees understand the roles they play and how their roles contribute to the objectives of the firm rests with the senior leadership team as it formulates and monitors strategy implementation.

Role of RPA in Step A: It has already been discussed that the RPA could have a major impact in the firm when it comes to the automation of highly repetitive and routine tasks. These tasks are ordinarily performed by knowledge workers. Since the RPA automates the highly repetitive and routine tasks, the benefits derived from it could include cost reduction, better accuracy, increased throughput and time efficiencies. Details of these benefits were discussed above. The RPA could be used to automate the process of assigning strategic responsibilities and objectives to the designated employees. Since the process is automated, it is able to track performance in an integrated manner and across the key strategic responsibilities and objectives assigned to relevant employees. The performance tracking occurs on an ongoing basis, timely and free of human intervention. Those charged with governance are able to harness this information and respond timely should the need arise to ensure that the strategic responsibilities and objectives assigned to relevant employees are on track. Table 7.1 illustrates a typical example of the firm that automates the processes of assigning strategic objectives and responsibilities to employees, as explored parallel to one that does not automate.

Step B: Alignment of structures and processes

Description of Step B: In strategy implementation, alignment of structures and processes should be a priority. In most cases, the plans, processes and structures of many firms operate in isolation, sometimes with little relationship even to firm strategy. For a firm to be able to implement strategy effectively, structures and processes need to be aligned with the strategic objectives. In the alignment of the

Table 7.2 Difference between two firms, one deploying RPA for automating processes and the other not

	Firm A	Firm B	Consequence	Competitive advantage
Application of RPA in key strategic processes	×	✓	The firm's strategy could be derailed if plans, processes and structures of the firm operate in isolation or are themselves isolated from the strategy	The firm applying RPA gains advantage of having a tool for eliminating human intervention, and integrating plans, processes and structures

Source: Authors' own illustration

structure of the firm to the strategic objectives, activities should be coordinated, and the skills and capabilities of the firm should be made available for the benefit of the firm. In addition, it is important to align the ongoing and proposed projects to strategic objectives. A full assessment and evaluation of the contribution of each project towards the strategic objectives will inform decisions such as which projects should be resourced and carried through to completion.

Role of RPA in Step B: The risk that could derail the strategy could emanate from plans, processes and structures that the firm operate in isolation or are themselves isolated from the strategy. RPA could be a major value addition when it comes to the automation and integration of these processes. Automated and integrated processes allow those charged with governance to track performance in an integrated manner and across the key strategic responsibilities and objectives assigned to relevant employees. Similarly, performance tracking will occur on an ongoing basis, timely and free of human intervention. RPA provides a tool for eliminating human intervention and for integrating plans, processes and structures. Table 7.2 illustrates a typical example of the firm that automates the processes of aligning the firm's structures and systems and another that does not.

Step C: Alignment of human capital

Description of Step C: Effective people management is an important issue in the successful implementation of a strategy. The contributions of all the employees of the firm should be aligned with the strategy of the firm. This alignment helps employees to align with the achievement of the firm's objectives. For the implementation to be successful, it is important that firms create a cohesive strategy that employees can understand and effectively engage with.

Role of RPA in Step C: We think the value of the RPA here will be the automation of the performance management system within the firm. Similar to A, the RPA could be used to automate the process of assigning strategic responsibilities and objectives to the designated employees. Since the process is automated, it is able to track performance in an integrated manner and across the key strategic responsibilities and objectives assigned to relevant employees. The performance tracking occurs on an ongoing basis, timely and free of human intervention. Those charged with governance are able to harness this information and respond timely should the need arise to ensure that the strategic responsibilities and objectives assigned to relevant

Table 7.3 Difference between two firms, one deploying RPA for automating processes and the other not

	Firm A	Firm B	Consequence	Competitive advantage
Application of RPA in key strategic processes	×	✓	The firm applying RPA in key strategic processes will be able to automate its performance management system and track performance in an integrated manner and across the key strategic responsibilities and objectives assigned to relevant employees	The firm applying RPA gains advantage as the performance tracking occurs on an ongoing basis, timely and free of human intervention. Those charged with governance are able to harness this information and respond timely should the need arise to ensure that the strategic responsibilities and objectives assigned to relevant employees are performed the way they were intended and are on track

Source: Authors' own illustration

employees are on track. Table 7.3 illustrates a typical example of the firm that automates the performance process, assigning and aligning the strategic objectives and responsibilities to employees, and of another that does not automate.

7.5 Key Points

- Robotics and RPA concepts are often confused. The confusion may be caused by the fact that there are some crossovers between robotics and RPA.
- Robots are used to automate physical tasks, such as in manufacturing.
- There are so many types of automation that have nothing to do with physical robots. There are so many branches of robotics that have nothing to do with automation.
- Robots have consistent characteristics including a certain form of mechanical aspect. This aspect helps the robot complete tasks in the environment for which it is designed. Robots would also need electrical components that control and power the machinery, and they would typically contain some form of computer programming.
- RPA can be viewed as bringing together business models, strategy, process, data, humans and robots. This is done in order to achieve efficiencies within the business processes.
- RPA has several benefits, including cost reduction, time efficiencies, better accuracy rate, improved governance environment, better customer advocacy

and retention, improved checks and balances, increased speed and productivity, easy integration into existing technologies and super-scalability.
- The firm applying RPA gains advantage as the performance tracking occurs on an ongoing basis, timely and free of human intervention. Those charged with governance are able to harness this information and respond timely should the need arise to ensure that the strategic responsibilities and objectives assigned to relevant employees are on track.
- The firm applying RPA also gains advantage of having a tool for eliminating human intervention and integrating plans, processes and structures.

References

van der Aalst, W. M. P., Bichler, M., & Heinzl, A. (2018). Robotic process automation. *Business and Information Systems Engineering, 60*, 269–272. https://doi.org/10.1007/s12599-018-0542-4.

Anagnoste, S. (2017). Robotic automation process-the next major revolution in terms of back office operations improvement. *Proceedings of the International Conference on Business Excellence, 11*(1), 676–686.

Boulton, C. (2018). *What is RPA? A revolution in business process automation*. Available from https://www.cio.com/article/3236451/what-is-rpa-robotic-process-automation-explained.html

Brooks, R. A. (1991). New approaches to robotics. *Science, 253*(5025), 1227–1232.

GRANTA. (2017). *What is the difference between automation and robotics*? Available from https://www.granta-automation.co.uk/news/what-is-the-difference-between-automation-and-robotics/

Howe, R. D., & Matsuoka, Y. (1999). Robotics for surgery. *Annual Review of Biomedical Engineering, 1*(1), 211–240.

Kober, J., Bagnell, J. A., & Peters, J. (2013). Reinforcement learning in robotics: A survey. *The International Journal of Robotics Research, 32*(11), 1238–1274.

Koren, Y., & Koren, Y. (1985). *Robotics for engineers*. New York: McGraw-Hill.

Nof, S. Y. (1999). *Handbook of industrial robotics*. New York: Wiley.

Owen-Hill, A. (2017). *What's the difference between automation and robotics*? Available from https://www.blog.robotiq.com/whats-the-diffrence-between-automation-and-robotics

PWC South Africa. (2020). *Robotic process automation*. Available from https://www.pwc.co.za/en/services/advisor/robotic-process-automation.html

Taylor, R. H., Menciassi, A., Fichtinger, G., Fiorini, P., & Dario, P. (2016). Medical robotics and computer-integrated surgery. In B. Siciliano & O. Khatib (Eds.), *Springer handbook of robotics* (Springer handbooks). Cham: Springer. https://doi.org/10.1007/978-3-319-32552-1_63.

Wiens, R. C., Maurice, S., & Rull Perez, F. (2017). The SuperCam remote sensing instrument suite for the Mars 2020 rover mission: A preview. *Spectroscopy, 32*. (LA-UR-17-26876).

Williford, K. H., Farley, K. A., Stack, K. M., Allwood, A. C., Beaty, D., Beegle, L. W., & Hecht, M. H. (2018). The NASA Mars 2020 rover mission and the search for extraterrestrial life. In *From habitability to life on Mars* (pp. 275–308). Amsterdam: Elsevier.

Yoshikawa, T. (1990). *Foundations of robotics: Analysis and control*. Massachusetts: MIT Press.

Synopsis to Artificial Intelligence and the Nature of a Firm: Implications to Strategy and Strategy Implementation

8

8.1 Introduction

In Chap. 1, it was indicated that before the COVID-19, the world was already changing rapidly. According to Birkinshaw (2018), AI already played a major role in assisting many firms to exploit their existing sources of advantage—whether through process automation, improved problem-solving or quality assurance. In essence, AI was beginning to be useful in exploring the new sources of advantage for firms.

As the world changed, Chap. 1 noted, it would seem that firms and individuals within those firms were caught between leveraging the advances brought about by technology and keeping certain aspects of the firm in a traditional form. For instance, in most companies, meetings had to be physically attended in the boardrooms, even though virtual meeting platforms were available for some time.

When the great pandemic (COVID-19) descended on humanity towards the end of 2019, most governments responded by confining their citizens due to the fear that the virus would spread and that the hospitals would not cope. Businesses such as gymnasiums, restaurants, nightclubs, bars and casinos all had to shut down or work with minimal staff members. Here, a difference emerged. Firms that did not necessarily require physical presence continued to operate under these circumstances. Meetings, workshops, or labs were swiftly moved to the virtual space. There has been an intense utilisation of technologies such as Google Meet, CISCO WEBEX, Zoom, Microsoft Teams, Skype, among other technologies. Firms moved to use technology intensely. Technology has become a trusted companion for most firms. Instead of human capital being the essential resource, suddenly, most firms could not do without technology.

The rock on which the firm had been initially thought and built was shifting. As previously articulated, the firm's nature had to be revisited, particularly the aspects of strategy and strategy implementation. Since long-term strategies require information, the ability of AI to harness massive amounts of data is an essential aspect of managing trade-offs, since certain scenarios may be uncertain.

T. Moloi, T. Marwala, *Artificial Intelligence and the Changing Nature of Corporations*, Future of Business and Finance,
https://doi.org/10.1007/978-3-030-76313-8_8

As the world becomes more complex and ever uncertain, instead of relying on human resources as an essential aspect of a firm's processes, there is a need to incorporate advanced data analytics in strategic planning and to incorporate advanced data analytics and some aspects of automating the strategy execution (business processes/operations).

8.2 Synopsis of Artificial Intelligence

In Chap. 2, we indicated that historically, AI came into the spotlight driven by the United Kingdom (UK) and the United States of America (USA). In 1950, Turing put together and published computing machinery and intelligence, which became a seminal work. In the USA, the concept of AI was inspired by science fiction known as runaround that was created by Isaac Asimov. The DSRPAI was an important convention which propelled AI a step forward. There were still challenges as early computers could not store commands; they only executed them. Another early challenge in the computing world is that computers were unaffordable.

Since these early developments, AI has grown in leaps and bounds. Various technologies exist currently, including the natural language generation (NLG), natural language understanding (NLU), speech recognition (SR), ML, virtual agents (VL), expert systems (ES), decision management (DM), deep learning (DL), robotic process automation (RPA), text analytics (TA), natural language processing (NLP), biometrics, cyber defense (CD), emotion recognition (ER) and image recognition (IR).

AI can be classified into strong and weak AI. The concept of weak and strong AI emanates from Searle's (1980) objection to the argument put forward by the proponents of the idea that the relation between the brain and the body of a human being is identical in many respects to the relation between the hardware and the software of AI and machine consciousness (MC).

8.3 Synopsis of a Firm's Strategy

Chapter 3 provided a high-level overview of strategy by discussing the historical account of strategy, followed by a discussion aimed at understanding the concept of the strategy. Chapter 3 further outlined and discussed processes that firms need to undertake as they formulate the strategy. From the discussions, it became apparent that strategy has long existed within living organisms. Strategy as a concept emanated from the need of the people to defeat their adversaries.

It was indicated that the concept of strategy could be traced back to the period between 200 B.C. and 400 B.C. Chapter 3 highlighted that the first text that emphasised strategy was the *Art of War* by Sun Tzu. This was written sometime between 400 B.C. and 500 B.C. From a business perspective, strategy refers to how firms explain to their stakeholders the ways in which they will be moving forward.

Firm strategy is generally viewed as a course of action that can help the firm attain its objectives.

Furthermore, Chap. 3 outlined three aspects of strategy formulation, namely, corporate-level strategy, competitive strategy (sometimes called the business strategy) and the parenting strategy. The growth or directional strategy outlines the growth objective of the firm, especially on how to achieve this growth. The portfolio strategy outlines the portfolio of the lines of the firm, which assist in the diversification that the business should engage in. The parenting strategy explains how resources are allocated and managed. It highlights which areas to emphasise. The strategy contains three phases, and these are the diagnosis, formulation and implementation phases.

8.4 Synopsis of Strategy and Strategy Implementation

Chapter 4 highlighted some key definitions of strategy implementation. This was followed by a brief distinction between strategy implementation and strategy execution. Some activities involved in strategy implementation were briefly outlined, and some factors that firms need to consider as they implement strategies were discussed. The chapter further outlined the typical pitfalls in strategy implementation and mitigations for successful strategy implementation.

The terms strategy implementation and strategy execution are sometimes used interchangeably, even though some researchers argue that these are different processes. Planning, organising, leadership and control are essential activities for strategy implementation. To implement the strategy successfully, firms need to have the right people. Firms need to allocate adequate resources to provide support to the business units to execute the strategy.

As firms consider strategy, the executive layer of the firm must define the lines of communication throughout the organisation. Firms further need to consider the systems, tools and capabilities that the firm has to facilitate the implementation of the strategies, and they will need to promote a culture of cooperation, responsibility and accountability.

8.5 Synopsis of Machine Learning

Chapter 5 provided an overview of the concept of ML. This was followed by a discussion of the growing influence of ML and the forms of ML were outlined. In addition, a brief overview of deep learning was introduced. The final part of the chapter explored ML in strategy and in strategy implementation.

It became apparent in the discussions that ML addresses the question of how to construct computers that are capable of improving automatically through experience. Over the years, ML has grown substantially. Its growth and progress could be attributable to online data availability and low-cost computation.

Chapter 5 indicated that three forms of ML exist, namely, supervised learning, unsupervised learning and reinforced learning. In addition, two types of learning exist, and these are deep learning (DL) and shallow learning (SL). SL would typically contain the single-layer neural networks, whereas DL would contain many layers of neural networks. DL requires more computation power for forward or backward optimisation while training, testing and eventually running these neural networks. DL often outperforms shallow ML methods, which often consist of single neural networks.

We propose various steps in strategy and strategy implementation to which the ML could be deployed. On the situational analysis of internal environment, we indicate that this would require that a firm process the stored internal data to extract value from it. These massive amount of data would ordinarily be complicated for the traditional methods. ML can take supervised learning, unsupervised learning and reinforcement learning forms as indicated earlier. The process includes data collection, data preparation, training, evaluation and tuning in all these types of learning. It is clear here that as algorithms receive data, they will learn and understand the firm better. What is further clear is that the stored internal data come in both structured and unstructured forms. These massive amounts of data are troublesome for traditional methods. The ability of ML to handle this type of data is important for a firm to uncover key trends and patterns within data to provide further insights that are crucial for crafting the mission, strategic objectives, strategies and desired results, and significant strengths and weaknesses.

Concerning the situation analysis on external environment, we indicate that this would require that a firm process the available external data to extract value from it. The data could come from industry sources, national and international statistical agencies, business news, securities exchange, news services, experts' opinions, etc. The massive volume of data required for evaluating and informing the mission, strategic objectives, strategies and major opportunities and threats of a firm would typically be complex if it were to be done manually and by a human being. As explained earlier, ML can take supervised learning, unsupervised learning and reinforcement learning. The typical process includes data collection, data preparation, training, evaluation and tuning in all these types of learning. It is clear here that as algorithms receive data, they will learn and understand the firm better. What is further clear is that the stored internal data come in both structured and unstructured modes. These massive amounts of data are troublesome and strictly speaking very time-consuming, if traditional methods are deployed. The abilities of ML to handle this type of data are important for a firm to uncover key trends and patterns within data to provide further insights that are crucial crafting the mission, strategic objectives, strategies and desired results, and significant opportunities and threats.

Regarding the objective setting process of the strategy and of strategy implementation, we note that this requires analysis of each factor that influences the selection of objectives and therefore will be a cumbersome process for traditional methods that have previously relied on human beings. Numerous factors could influence the selection of objectives. Each of them has to be assessed, analysed and considered for a decision to be taken. These are many datasets, with which ML is wired to deal for the formulation of potential scenarios that could then be analysed, and the best option chosen. Objectives emanating from a data-intensive and data-informed process are risk-calibrated since several factors that influence the selection of objectives would have been considered.

Concerning the analysis of internal and external environments, we indicate that ML is wired to deal with Big Data, which would otherwise be a cumbersome process for a human being or traditional methods. The analysis of general economic and industrial environments in which the firm operates, competition and its manoeuvres as well as the firm's strengths, weaknesses, threats and opportunities require massive data handling, labelling and integration to formulate potential scenarios. The ability of ML to handle massive data is important for a firm to uncover key trends and patterns within data; it is also important for insights into data, which are crucial in a firm's formulation of potential scenarios.

Setting targets requires that the firm understand its key stakeholder needs. The firm will formulate the strategic objectives. Each objective is translated into goals, which subsequently address the firm's key stakeholder needs. The firm's operations would rely on each other to ensure that the bigger goal is achieved. The finance department relies on the sales department to drive the sales, and in turn, the sales department will rely on the finance department to ensure that marketing and advertising invoices are paid on time, and that finance provides it with management accounts to see how far it is from its targets. This example would typically represent the firm's internal interdependencies. External stakeholders such as customers also need to be understood, for example, the questions of what product they are learning towards, what informs such a view and what does that mean for a firm. The ML user modelling platforms could be used to mine data of this nature, which could subsequently allow a firm to make an informed decision.

Similar to the target setting, the segmentation of plans requires an understanding of what each segment is capable of (segment capabilities). It further requires an understanding of segment dependencies. To formulate this understanding, a firm requires many structured and unstructured datasets that ML is wired to deal with for the understanding of capabilities and dependencies. The segmentation of plans emanating from a data-intensive and data-informed process are risk-calibrated based on the capabilities and dependencies of a firm.

The performance review step requires that data to be analysed to pick up the gaps between the desired and the actual goals. Big Data will provide insights relating to the factors that have contributed to the achievement or non-achievement of the desired performance. The decision can then be made as to where resources need to be ploughed to improve performance or to leverage the process so that it yields even better results. Automated systems are also able to report the performance in real time. Should senior leadership wish to see performance at a certain period, they need not wait for reporting timelines.

Strategic choice will be a function of understanding vast sets of data, which are converted to information by ML Algorithms. This includes internal and external contexts, macro-economic factors, the industry in which the company operates, the strengths, weaknesses, opportunities, threats, interdependencies, key internal and external stakeholders, behaviour of competitors, behaviour of clients, targets and performance measures among other key things. On the implementation process, data are analysed to pick up the gaps between the mission, values and vision. The data could come from various sources that speak to the firm's value system, mission and vision. The data will be both structured and unstructured. Mapping the data to ensure that there is alignment to these three crucial aspects of strategy could be time-consuming if traditional methods are deployed. The ability of ML to handle this type of data is important for a firm to uncover key trends and patterns within data to provide further insights that are crucial in aligning the mission, vision and values. On building effective leadership, we see the role of ML as the provision of key insights relating to the factors contributing to the achievement of the desired performance. Performance information coming through from operations indicates where resources need to be ploughed to improve performance or to leverage the process so that it yields even better results. This requires that the firm has access to the information on an ongoing basis, and that it has a nimble style of leadership. Nimble leadership refers to the leadership that allows for the adjustment of certain positions, should data point to the need of such an adjustment. Automated systems are also crucial in reporting performance in real time. Should senior leadership wish to see performance, at a certain period, they need not wait for reporting timelines.

Creating the overarching implementation plan is important for the identification of resources required and the steps that need to be followed to achieve the goals. Data are analysed to understand the financial resources, personnel, operational and technological resources required. These data are also quantified. The data could come from various sources, and it has to speak to the priorities, accountabilities and the short-term and long-term objectives of the firm. The data will be both structured and unstructured. Mapping these data to ensure that there is life to the implementation plan could otherwise be time-consuming if traditional methods are deployed. The abilities of ML to handle this type of data is important for a firm to uncover key trends and patterns within data to provide further insights, which are crucial in identifying key priorities, accountabilities and the short-term and long-term objectives of the firm.

The step on allocation of budgetary resources was noted to be similar to creation of the implementation plans, as the achievement of the overarching implementation plan hinges on the identification of resources required and the steps that need to be followed to achieve the goals. Data are analysed and quantified to understand the financial resources. There could be various sources of data. The allocation of financial resources has to be guided by the firm's priorities in the short term and long term. The data will be structured and unstructured. Mapping these data to ensure that there is life to the implementation plan could otherwise be time-consuming if traditional methods are deployed. The ability of ML to handle this type of data is important for a firm to uncover key trends and patterns within data to provide further insights, which are crucial in identifying key priorities and budgetary requirements in the short term and long term.

On assigning roles and responsibilities, we previously indicated that strategic choice would be a function of understanding vast sets of data, which are converted to information by ML Algorithms. Similarly, the allocation of responsibilities to various individuals will be a function of understanding vast data, including capabilities and interdependencies of various key individuals driving the strategy within the firm. Additional data could include the internal and external context, macro-economic factors, the industry in which the company operates, the strengths, weaknesses, opportunities, threats, interdependencies, key internal and external stakeholders, behaviour of competitors, behaviour of clients, targets and performance measures among other key things. On aligning structures and processes, we indicated that the strategic choice would be a function of understanding vast sets of data, which are converted to information by ML Algorithms. Similarly, the alignment of structures and processes of different segments will be a function of understanding vast data, including capabilities and interdependencies of various key segments driving strategy within the firm. Misalignments could lead to the failure of the segment to perform, which could affect other segments. We see the role of ML as that of provision of key insights relating to the key processes and structures that contribute to the achievement of the desired performance.

The alignment of human capital requires that data be analysed to understand the contribution of each team player to the desired goal. Big Data will provide insights relating to the factors that could contribute to the team player failing to contribute to the achievement or non-achievement of the desired performance. The decision can then be made as to where resources need to be ploughed to improve performance or to leverage the process so that it yields even better results.

On communicating the strategy, we indicated that the automated systems are also able to report the performance of a team player in real time. Should senior leadership wish to see the performance of a team player at a certain time frame, they need not wait for the performance review period. They are able to access this, and correct any deviation on an ongoing basis. The main advantage of the technology-driven tools is that they are digital. Critical points that the senior leadership needs to communicate across the group could be communicated through the digital tools. We indicated that ML could take supervised learning, unsupervised learning and reinforcement learning. The process includes data collection, data preparation, training, evaluation and tuning in all these types of learning. As algorithms receive data, they will learn and understand the data and the intended outcomes better. What is further clear is that the stored internal data come in both structured and unstructured modes. These massive amounts of data are troublesome for traditional methods. The ability of ML to handle this type of data is important for a firm to uncover key trends and patterns within data to provide further insights, which are crucial in eliminating any ambiguity.

In relation to tracking the performance, we indicated that data are analysed to pick up the gaps between desired and actual goals. Big Data will provide insights relating to factors that have contributed to the achievement or non-achievement of the desired performance. This is important in checking whether the strategy is implemented as envisaged. The decision can then be made as to where resources need to be ploughed to improve performance or to leverage the process so that it yields even better results. Automated systems are also able to report the performance in real time. Should senior leadership wish to see performance at a certain period, they need not wait for reporting timelines.

8.6 Synopsis of Natural Language Processing

Chapter 6 discussed the concept of NLP. This was followed by a discussion of how the NLP is applied. The chapter further outlined the typical functions of the NLP. Finally, the chapter explored NLP in relation to strategy and strategy implementation. It was indicated that the NLP is a branch of computer science, AI and linguistics that focuses on the interaction between computer programmes and human language.

Furthermore, there are three functions of the NLP, namely, machine translation (MT), text summarisation and sentiment analysis (SA). MT is a branch of computer linguistics that analyses computerised tools to translate the context derived from this, from one language to the next. The language that is being translated is the human language.

Automatic text summarisation refers to a process of bringing about a succinct and meaningful summary of the text. SA is a way of finding out the polarity or strength of the opinion that is expressed in the written text. The opinion could be positive or negative. MT has three significant approaches, and these are rule-based MT, statistical MT and neural MT. A rule-based system would typically require the expert to know both the source and target languages. This knowledge is then used to develop syntactic, semantic and morphological rules to achieve the translation.

The statistical approach uses statistical models based on the analysis of bilingual text corpora. The neural MT approach uses neural networks to achieve machine translation. There are two broad categories of text summarisation approaches, namely, extractive and abstractive summarisation. In addition, there are four popular types of SA, inclusive of the fine-grained SA, emotion detection, aspect-based SA and multilingual SA.

We propose various steps in strategy and strategy implementation for the deployment of NLP and ML. On the situational analysis of internal environment, we conclude that it would require that a firm process the stored internal data to extract value from it. The massive volume of spoken data required to evaluate and inform the mission, strategic objectives, strategies and strengths and weaknesses of a firm would typically be complex if it were to be done manually and by a human being. The NLP has two main applications: speech recognition (SR) and speech synthesis (SS). Once the algorithms are trained to recognise or synthesise a particular language, then it can be exported to the ML. It is clear here that as the ML algorithms receive data exported from the NLP, they will better understand the firm. What is further clear is that the stored internal data come in both structured and unstructured forms. These massive amounts of data are troublesome for traditional methods. The ability of ML to handle this type of data is important for a firm to uncover key trends and patterns within data in order to provide further insights, which are crucial for crafting the mission, strategic objectives, strategies, desired results and significant strengths and weaknesses.

On the situational analysis of the external environment, we conclude that it would require that a firm process the available external data to extract value from it. The data could come from industry sources, national and international statistical agencies, business news, securities exchange, news services, experts' opinions, etc. These could come in the form of spoken language, i.e., interviews. Speech recognition (SR) and speech synthesis (SS) could then be deployed to extract, recognise or synthesise these data. Once the algorithms are trained to recognise or synthesise a particular language, then it can be exported to the ML. The massive volume of data required to evaluate and inform the mission, strategic objectives, strategies and major opportunities and threats of a firm would typically be complex if it were to be done manually and by a human being. As explained earlier, ML can take the supervised learning, unsupervised learning and reinforcement learning forms. The typical process includes data collection, data preparation, training, evaluation and tuning in all these types of learning. It is clear here that as algorithms receive data, they will learn and understand the firm better. What is further clear is that the stored internal data come in both structured and unstructured forms. These massive amounts of data are troublesome and very time-consuming if traditional methods are deployed. The ability of ML to handle this type of data is important for a firm to uncover key trends and patterns within data to provide further insights, which are crucial in crafting the mission, strategic objectives, strategies and desired results, and significant opportunities and threats.

On objective setting, analysis of each factor that influences the selection of objectives will be a cumbersome process for traditional methods that have previously relied on human beings. There are potentially numerous factors influencing the selection of objectives. The selection of objectives could happen in a boardroom, in which various factors are evaluated and considered. Each of the factors put forward has to be assessed, analysed and considered for a decision to be taken. This involves the spoken language a lot. Speech recognition (SR) and speech synthesis (SS) could then be deployed to extract, recognise or synthesise these data. Once the algorithms are trained to recognise or synthesise a particular language, then it can be exported to the ML. ML is wired to deal with these many datasets to formulate potential scenarios that could then be analysed, and the best option chosen. Objectives emanating from the data-intensive and data-informed process are risk-calibrated, as several factors that influence the selection of objectives would have been considered.

With regard to the analysis of the internal and external contexts, the general economic and industrial environment in which the firm operates, the competition and its movement and the firm's strengths, weaknesses threats and opportunities could come from industry experts, and in the form of a human language. Speech recognition (SR) and speech synthesis (SS) could then be deployed to extract, recognise or synthesise these data. Once the algorithms are trained to recognise a particular language or synthesise it, then it can be exported to the ML. The abilities of ML to handle massive data are important for a firm to uncover key trends and patterns within data, which is important for insights into data. These insights are crucial in assisting a firm as it formulates potential scenarios.

We indicate that target setting requires that the firm understand its key stakeholders' needs. There is a need for a firm to lend an ear to stakeholders, particularly when it comes to external stakeholders such as customers or investors, as needs can be expressed in investor conferences, annual conferences or customer service platforms using a spoken language. We previously indicated that each objective is translated into goals that subsequently address the firm's key stakeholder needs. External stakeholders such as customers also need to be understood, in relation to what product they are leaning towards, what informs such a view and what that means for a firm. Speech recognition (SR) and speech synthesis (SS) could then be deployed to extract, recognise or synthesise these data, if they are in a natural language. Once the algorithms are trained to recognise or synthesise a particular language, then it can be exported to the ML. The ML user modelling platforms could be used to mine data of this nature, allowing a firm to make an informed decision.

Concerning the performance review process, we observe that market commentators would provide an in-depth analysis of the firm's performance against the desired targets. In most cases, the senior leadership presents the results to the shareholders. These presentations are in a natural language format. Sometimes questions are raised and answers are provided, all in a natural language. This step requires that data be analysed to identify the gaps between desired and actual goals. Big Data will provide insights relating to the factors that have contributed to the achievement or non-achievement of the desired performance. The decision can then be made as to where resources need to be ploughed to improve performance or leverage the process to yield even better results. Speech recognition (SR) and speech synthesis (SS) could then be deployed to extract, recognise or synthesise these data if they are in a natural language. Once the algorithms are trained to recognise or synthesise a particular language, then it can be exported to the ML.

In relation to making strategic choice, we indicate that huge datasets play a huge role. This includes internal and external contexts, macro-economic factors, the industry in which the company operates, the strengths, weaknesses, opportunities, threats, interdependencies, key internal and external stakeholders, behaviour of competitors, behaviour of clients, targets and performance measures among other key things. Some of this key information is provided by market commentators, analysts, investors and financial institutions in a natural language. Speech recognition (SR) and speech synthesis (SS) could then be deployed to extract, recognise or synthesise these data, if they are in a natural language. Once the algorithms are trained to recognise a particular language or synthesise it, then it can be exported to the ML.

Concerning using NLP in communication, we observe that communication could take verbal or written form. Sometimes, firms will use verbal communication, for instance, in executive committee meetings, team meetings, general meetings or meetings with shareholders. The main advantage of the technology-driven tools is that they are digital. Critical points that the senior leadership needs to communicate across the group could still be communicated verbally but captured through the digital tools. Communication from external stakeholders could be done verbally but captured through digital tools. Speech recognition (SR) and speech synthesis (SS) could then be deployed to extract, recognise or synthesise these data they are in a natural language. Once the algorithms are trained to recognise or synthesise a particular language, then it can be exported to the ML. We indicated that ML could take supervised learning, unsupervised learning and reinforcement learning form. The process includes data collection, data preparation, training, evaluation and tuning in all the types of learning. As algorithms receive data, they will learn and understand the data and the intended outcomes better. What is further evidence is that the stored internal data come in both structured and unstructured ways. These massive amounts of data are troublesome for traditional methods. The ability of ML to handle this type of data is essential for a firm to uncover key trends and patterns within data to provide further insights, which are crucial in eliminating any ambiguity.

8.7 Synopsis of Robotic Process Automation

Chapter 7 discussed the concept of robotics. A discussion of the RPA followed this. The benefits of the RPA were also outlined. The chapter further explored the RPA in relation to strategy and strategy implementation. It was clear that the robotics and RPA concepts are often confused, and the confusion may be caused by the fact that there are some crossovers between robotics and RPA.

Robots are used to automate physical tasks such as those found in manufacturing operations. So many types of automation have nothing to do with physical robots, and so many branches of robotics have nothing to do with automation. Robots have consistent characteristics, including a particular form of mechanical aspect. The mechanical aspect of a robot is fundamental in its quest to complete tasks that are in an environment for which it is designed. Robots would also need electrical components that control and power the machinery, and they would typically contain some forms of computer programming.

RPA can be viewed as bringing together business models, strategy, process, data, humans and robots. This is done in order to achieve efficiencies within the business processes. RPA has several benefits, including cost reduction, time efficiencies, better accuracy rate, improved governance environment, better customer advocacy and retention, improved checks and balances, increased speed and productivity, easy integration into existing technologies and super-scalability.

There are three steps in strategy and strategy implementation that we propose could be automated through the RPA. These are assignment of objectives and responsibilities, alignment of structures and processes and human capital alignment. We see the role of RPA in the assignment of objectives and responsibilities as that of automation of processes for assigning strategic responsibilities and objectives to the designated employees. Since the process is automated, the RPA will track performance in an integrated manner and across the key strategic responsibilities and objectives assigned to relevant employees. Performance tracking occurs on an ongoing basis, timely and free of human intervention. Those charged with governance can harness the performance information to assess whether the firm is still on track or not, then respond timely should the need arise to ensure that the strategic responsibilities and objectives assigned to relevant employees are on track.

On the alignment of structures and processes, we submit that the risk that could derail the strategy could emanate from plans, processes and structures that operate in isolation or are isolated from the strategy. An RPA process could add a significant value in the automation and integration of firm's structures and processes. Automated and integrated processes allow those charged with governance to track performance in an integrated manner and across key strategic responsibilities and objectives assigned to relevant employees. Similar to the above, performance tracking will occur on an ongoing basis, timely and free of human intervention. RPA provides a tool for eliminating human intervention and integrating plans, processes and structures.

About the alignment of human capital, we hold that the value of the RPA here will be the automation of the performance management system within the firm. Similarly, the RPA could be used to automate assigning of strategic responsibilities and objectives to the designated employees. Since the process is automated, it can track performance in an integrated manner and across key strategic responsibilities and objectives assigned to relevant employees. Performance tracking occurs on an ongoing basis, timely and free of human intervention. An RPA process can be beneficial to those charged with governance, as the integration and automation of processes would permit them to monitor the real time performance, and respond accordingly to ensure that the strategic responsibilities and objectives assigned to different employees are on track.

References

Birkinshaw, J. (2018). What's the purpose of companies in the age of AI? *Harvard Business Review*. Available from https://hbr.org/2018/08/whats-the-purpose-of-companies-in-the-age-of-ai

Searle, J. R. (1980). Minds, brains and programs. *Behavioral and Brain Sciences, 3*, 417–457.6.

Index

T. Moloi, T. Marwala, *Artificial Intelligence and the Changing Nature of Corporations*, Future of Business and Finance,
https://doi.org/10.1007/978-3-030-76313-8

The manufacturer's authorised representative in the EU is Springer Nature Customer Service Centre GmbH, Europaplatz 3, 69115 Heidelberg, Germany. If you have any concerns regarding our products, please contact ProductSafety@springernature.com

Printed and bound by CPI Group (UK) Ltd, Croydon, CR0 4YY
28/09/2026
02224070-0013